STATUS OF FUNDING UNDER PRIVATE PENSION PLANS

Pension Research Council

PENSION RESEARCH COUNCIL PUBLICATIONS

Status of Funding under Private Pension Plans

by

FRANK L. GRIFFIN, Jr.
Vice President and Actuary
The Wyatt Company

and

CHARLES L. TROWBRIDGE
Vice President and Chief Actuary
Bankers Life Company

Published for the
Pension Research Council
Wharton School of Finance and Commerce
University of Pennsylvania

by
RICHARD D. IRWIN, INC., Homewood, Illinois
IRWIN-DORSEY LIMITED, Georgetown, Ontario

PURPOSE OF THE COUNCIL

The Pension Research Council of the Wharton School of Finance and Commerce was created in 1952 for the purpose of sponsoring objective research in the area of private pensions. It was formed in response to the urgent need for a better understanding of the private pension movement. Private pensions have experienced a phenomenal growth during the last three decades, but their economic, political, and social implications are yet to be explored. They seem destined to play a major role in the quest for old-age economic security, but the nature of that role can be ascertained only on the basis of more enlightened evaluation of the capabilities and limitations of the private pension mechanism. It was to conduct an impartial study into the facts and basic issues surrounding private pensions, under the auspices of an academic and professional group representing leadership in every phase of the field, that the Council was organized.

Projects undertaken by the Council are broad in scope and predominantly interpretive rather than technical in nature. In general, attention is concentrated on areas which are not the object of special investigation by other research groups. Its research studies are conducted by mature scholars drawn from both the academic and business spheres. Research results are published from time to time in a series of books and monographs.

PARTICIPATING FIRMS

Alexander and Alexander, Inc.
Bankers Life Company
George B. Buck
Connecticut General Life Insurance Company
Connecticut Mutual Life Insurance Company
Continental Assurance Company
Daskais and Walls, Inc.
Equitable Life Assurance Society of the United States
Harold Faggen Associates
Flynn, Harrison and Conroy
A. S. Hansen, Inc.
Hewitt Associates
Huggins and Company
John Hancock Mutual Life Insurance Company
Johnson and Higgins
Lybrand, Ross Brothers and Montgomery
Marsh and McLennan
Metropolitan Life Insurance Company
Milliman and Robertson, Inc.
Mutual Life Insurance Company of New York
Peat, Marwick, Mitchell and Company
Pacific Mutual Life Insurance Company
Pension Planning Company, Inc.
Provident Mutual Life Insurance Company
Prudential Insurance Company of America
John St. John
Seefurth-McGiveran Corporation
Conrad Siegel
George V. Stennes and Associates
Ron Stever and Company
David G. Stone, Inc.
Towers, Perrin, Forster and Crosby, Inc.
The Wyatt Company

FOREWORD

The Pension Research Council has had a long and continuing interest in the security of the legitimate benefit expectations of participants in private pension plans. In 1958, it initiated a five-year study of the legal, financial, actuarial, and regulatory environment in which private pension plans operate in an effort to assess in a general way the prospects that the benefit expectations of pension plan participants would be realized. This study resulted in the publication of five volumes. The general conclusion of the study was that there were elements in the overall pension environment that could lead to the nonfulfillment of pension promises. The emphasis was on the conditions that *could* lead to frustration of benefit expectations rather than the development of statistical or other evidence that benefit expectations were, in fact, being frustrated. Especial concern was expressed that employers and other plan sponsors might not be following financial practices that would assure the meeting of benefit obligations.

The questions raised in the study were disturbing to many persons associated with the private pension movement, some of whom sought to develop objective evidence that would either substantiate the concerns expressed in the study or show them to be groundless. In an effort to shed light on the vital area of funding, Frank L. Griffin, Jr., vice president of The Wyatt Company in charge of its Chicago office and an internationally recognized expert on pension plans, examined the relationship between the assets and the actuarial liabilities of the pension plans serviced by his office that had been in process of funding for 10 years or more. The results of his investigation, which showed an eminently satisfactory level of funding, were presented in a paper before the 1964 Annual Meeting of the Conference of Actuaries in Public Practice. More important than the specific findings of this limited investigation was the methodology developed by Mr. Griffin to measure the funding progress of the plans included in his survey. He computed the market value of the pension plan assets and expressed it as a percentage of the single sum value of the accrued benefits. He termed this relationship the "benefit security ratio."

The Pension Research Council quickly sensed that application of the Griffin methodology to a representative sample of the private pension universe could provide meaningful insights into the financial aspects of benefit security and serve as a fitting sequel to the Council's earlier study of the qualitative elements of pension security. Mr. Griffin, whose firm is identified with trust fund plans, was consulted about such a study and ultimately agreed to undertake the more extensive investigation if a suitable representative of the life insurance companies could be persuaded to serve as co-director of the study. Charles L. Trowbridge, vice president and chief actuary of Bankers Life Company and author of classic actuarial papers on pension funding, consented to collaborate with Mr. Griffin, and the project was underway.

The study was limited to nongovernmental plans in process of funding for 10 years or more and covering at least 25 employees. These constraints were adopted in order to keep the number of cases within manageable bounds and to exclude those plans which on any reasonable standard of funding could not be expected to have funded in full, or in substantial part, the initial supplemental liability.

The central item of information sought with respect to these plans was the actuarial value of the accrued benefits. These values, computed with rate factors representative of those being quoted at the time by the leading life insurance companies, were to be compared to the respective asset accumulations to derive the benefit security ratio (BSR) for each plan in the study and for various classifications of plans. This approach was based on the premise that the relationship as of any given date between the assets of a pension plan and the actuarial value of its accrued benefit obligations serves as the most relevant and easily understood measure of the security attaching to such benefit accruals as of that time. Furthermore, the approach makes possible valid comparisons on a reasonably uniform basis of the funding progress under plans having heterogeneous characteristics and employing diverse actuarial cost methods as a guide to funding policy. To make the results even more meaningful, Messrs. Griffin and Trowbridge developed some benchmarks, arbitrary but realistic, that indicate at various durations the level of funding that might obtain under typical patterns of funding. As a further measure, plan assets were compared to the actuarial value of *vested* accrued benefits, the relationship being referred to as the VBSR.

The raw materials for the study were in the files of the actuarial consulting firms and life insurance companies that service the plans involved. Thus, it was necessary to enlist the cooperation of these firms. An appeal to participate in the project went out to the consulting firms and life insurance companies believed to be associated with the bulk of the plans falling within the purview of the study. Many found it impossible or impracticable to participate because of the demands that would be placed upon their technical staff, already overburdened with their normal operating responsibilities. Several life insurance companies were unable to provide information concerning pension plans funded through individual life insurance or annuity contracts, which by their structure normally generate an adequate level of funding. A few firms refused to participate because of reservations about the value of the study or the methodology to be employed. Ultimately, 22 consulting firms and 11 life insurance companies submitted data for the study. These organizations are listed immediately preceding this Foreword.

In order to broaden the base of participation and to identify subgroups of plans that might lend themselves to sampling, the data gathering was divided into two phases. The first phase sought information of a general nature that would give a clear profile of the plans under study and that could be supplied with minimum effort by the cooperating firms. This phase, which was virtually completed by the end of 1966, produced data on 3,983 plans, in all size categories and with the full range of relevant characteristics. These plans accounted for more than 9 million participants, about 44 percent of the estimated coverage of plans in existence for 10 years or more at the time of reporting. Phase I submissions were received for approximately one half of the plans in the universe having 5,000 or more participants, ranging down to about one tenth of the plans covering between 25 and 100 participants. There was underrepresentation of collectively bargained multiemployer plans and the smaller (fewer than 100 participants) single-employer plans.

The second phase called for special actuarial valuations and other data that could be provided only at great expense and inconvenience to the cooperating organizations. To minimize the work and expense involved, Phase II information was sought for only a sample of the Phase I plans rather than for all. Participating firms were asked to submit the requested information with respect to all plans covering 5,000 or more employees, one half of the plans covering 500 to 4,999 employees, and one fourth of the plans covering fewer than 500 employees, the plans for the sample being selected at random. The sampling procedure followed was expected to produce a sample of 1,161 plans, when account was taken of the fact

that a few firms which had supplied data for the first phase
of the study had given notice that they would not be able to
furnish the Phase II data. For various reasons, the special
valuations could not be carried out for some of these plans
and Phase II data were eventually received for 1,047 plans,
covering a total of 4,562,000 employees. The coverage of these
plans amounted to approximately one fourth of the universe.
The second phase of the data gathering was concluded by the
end of 1967.

Verification and analysis of the data began long before
the final Phase II reports had been submitted. A summary of
the principal findings was made available to the Pension Research Council in April, 1968. In recognition of the intense
interest of business and governmental groups in the study, the
Council authorized dissemination of the summary findings
prior to publication of the full report. A preliminary draft of
the complete report was reviewed by the Council at its October,
1968, meeting, and the final manuscript sent to the printer in
late November, 1968.

This was a mammoth undertaking, fraught with technical
and practical difficulties. Great credit for its successful conclusion is due to the many individuals and organizations who
joined forces to make the project a reality. The study could
not have been carried out without the splendid cooperation of
the firms that submitted the basic data, usually at substantial
out-of-pocket expense and always with disruption of normal
operating routines. The Council and the entire pension com-
munity are greatly in the debt of these firms for their public-
spirited action.

A special debt is owed to The Wyatt Company. This
organization not only submitted the largest number of cases
to the study; it also developed the computer program to analyze
the data and then processed the data on its computer facilities.
The computer program was developed by David Crawford,

A.S.A., of the Chicago office of The Wyatt Company who, with the able assistance of Mrs. Margo Engelhardt Voltin of the Chicago office, cleansed the data of reporting errors and monitored the entire computer operation. Mr. Crawford and Mrs. Voltin devoted their full time to the project for several months and made an absolutely invaluable contribution to its success. Their services were provided free of charge by The Wyatt Company and only a nominal charge was made for use of the computer facilities. Finally, the organization contributed the services of Frank Griffin as co-director of the study.

The financial strain on the cooperating firms was significantly reduced by a grant of $169,500 to the Council by the Social Security Administration in support of the project. The grant enabled the Council to offer partial reimbursement to the firms for their out-of-pocket expenses, greatly enhancing the feasibility of the study which involved costs of at least a half million dollars. The Council records its deep appreciation to the Social Security Administration for its generous support and its approbation of the work of the Council.

The greatest debt is owed to the co-directors of the study, Frank Griffin and C. L. Trowbridge, who are also the authors of this volume. These individuals, both members of the Pension Research Council, are busy executives, burdened with manifold responsibilities, and yet they found time to devote months of intensive efforts to the project. Their approach to the project was in the best traditions of academic research, never tinged with partisan interests. Their techniques were scholarly, their analyses objective, and their conclusions consistent with the findings. They can truly be proud of the end product which will undoubtedly be regarded as a landmark in pension research and can be expected to serve as a model for similar efforts in the future.

The findings of this study are eloquent testimony to the conscientiousness with which employers and other plan sponsors have attempted to make financial provision for their accruing pension obligations. The results suggest that pension plans in general are currently in sound financial condition. Yet this is only a one-time snapshot of the financial condition of the plans, and the situation can be expected to change, for better or worse, as time goes on and circumstances change. As is pointed out by the directors of the study, the funding status as of any given moment in time, while significant, is not nearly as important as the direction in which the funding is moving. The goal may be a dollar of pension assets for every dollar of actuarial liability for accrued benefits, but in the long run the goal is probably unattainable. The important thing is that there be steady progress, notwithstanding temporary setbacks, toward the goal. This progress can be measured only if the type of study represented by this project is repeated at periodic intervals. It is hoped that this study will serve as a stimulus to plan administrators to request a termination-of-plan valuation of accrued benefit obligations as a routine procedure, possibly each time a normal valuation is carried out. This practice would not only provide additional guidance to plan administrators in the setting of funding policy but could lead to more meaningful financial reporting to plan participants. Not least important, it would make it possible to undertake, on a more comprehensive scale and at less expense, studies of this type on a periodic basis, as a guide to public policy.

April, 1969   DAN M. MCGILL
                                 Chairman and
                                 Research Director

TABLE OF CONTENTS

LIST OF TABLES AND CHARTS

Chapter 1

Introduction and Summary

This introductory chapter presents an "overview" of the entire funding study. It is designed to provide, in advance of the presentation of technical detail and plan breakdowns, a basic understanding of the problems inherent in such a funding inquiry, the techniques required to obtain meaningful results, the nature of the plans included in the study, and the significance of the findings. These matters are treated more fully in subsequent chapters.

Purposes of Study

The primary purpose of this study has been to determine the degree to which funding of accrued benefits has thus far been accomplished under a large segment of the private pension plans in the United States. A secondary purpose has been to examine current vesting practices and to ascertain the extent to which the values of accrued benefits are vested (i.e., the extent to which ultimate payment is not contingent upon an employee's continuing in the service of the employer).

Collection of Data

A total of 47 actuarial consulting firms and insurance companies were invited to participate in the study. The reporting instructions issued to the 33 firms and companies which accepted the invitation are shown in the Appendix. All reports were reviewed and edited for internal consistency and, wherever necessary, corrected on the basis of further correspondence with the reporting company. Information was transferred to punched cards; details relating to the actuarial calculations were later transferred to tape for processing.

The study was divided into two parts for data collection purposes, Part I consisting of a questionnaire identifying the principal plan characteristics of all plans within the group defined for the study, and Part II summarizing the results of special actuarial calculations which were made for a designated subsample of the Part I cases.

The Plans Studied

Plans included in the study are advance funded,[1] in almost all cases IRS qualified,[2] pension plans maintained for employees by private employers in the United States, which at the time of the study covered at least 25 participants and had been in process of funding for 10 or more years.

Not included in the study are (1) profit-sharing or savings plans (which, while they may provide accumulations for retirement purposes, are not pension plans in the usual sense) and (2) pension plans covering public employees (i.e., employees of federal, state, or local governments or their agencies). The fact that unfunded plans, which provide the lowest degree of benefit security, are not included should be kept in mind.

---

[1] Assets for the ultimate payment of pensions accumulated in advance of the date such payments fall due, under an insurance contract or in a fund outside the control of the employer.

[2] That is, "nondiscriminatory" according to IRS rules and thus qualified for tax deduction of employer contributions and other tax treatment appropriate to such plans. The nature of some employer organizations whose plans may have been included is such as not to require tax qualification.

The plans reported contain an impressively large proportion of the total number of participants under single-employer plans, which account for the bulk of private pension plan coverage in the United States, as well as a substantial number of participants under multiemployer plans, both Taft–Hartley[3] and other types. Altogether 3,983 plans were reported for Part I, covering 9,114,000 participants. A total of 1,047 plans were included in the Part II actuarial calculations, covering 4,562,000 participants and having at the time of valuation total assets of $22.2 billions.

The following table sets forth an estimate of the number of participants in the "universe" of funded private pension plans, together with the number of participants included in Parts I and II of the study. The estimate of the "universe" was derived from information contained in the following publications:

"Ten Years of Employee-Benefit Plans," by Alfred M. Skolnik, April 1966, Social Security Bulletin.

"Growth of Employee-Benefit Plans, 1954–61," by Alfred M. Skolnik, April 1963, Social Security Bulletin.

Letter from Robert J. Myers (Chief Actuary, Social Security Administration) to Frank L. Griffin, Jr., dated April 10, 1967.

"Private and Public Pension Plans in the United States," March 1967, Institute of Life Insurance.

Life Insurance Fact Book (1968).

Employee Benefit Plan Review: RESEARCH REPORTS, 101–13.

Measurements of Funding Employed

This funding inquiry has been conducted in terms of the relationship between the value of pension plan assets and the

---

[3] The term "Taft–Hartley plan" as used herein means a plan set up under a collective bargaining agreement, covering employees of several independent employers, which satisfies the requirements of Section 302(c) (5) of the Labor Management Relations Act.

TABLE 1-1

COMPARISON OF NUMBERS OF PARTICIPANTS IN THE PRIVATE PENSION UNIVERSE
WITH PARTICIPANTS INCLUDED IN PENSION RESEARCH COUNCIL STUDY
(In Millions)

	Approximate Number of Private Pension Plan Participants (Active and Retired) in 1966		
	"Universe"* (End of 1966)	Part I Sample†	Part II Subsample‡
Under Plans Adopted since 1956			
Taft–Hartley plans	1.3	Not In Study	
All other plans	4.7		
Total	6.0		
Under Plans Adopted 1956 or Earlier			
Taft–Hartley plans	3.0	0.9	0.2
All other plans	17.6	8.2	4.4
Total	20.6	9.1	4.6
Totals			
Taft–Hartley plans	4.3	0.9	0.2
All other plans	22.3	8.2	4.4
Total	26.6	9.1	4.6

* Not including persons whose "pension" coverage is limited to participation in deferred profit-sharing plans, estimated to number approximately 3 million. The total of 26.6 million private pension plan participants (exclusive of those covered solely by profit-sharing plans) is thus in close agreement with the estimate of 29.5 million participants under all types of retirement program, as reported in Life Insurance Fact Book (1968). Figures here illustrated are believed to include about 400,000 pension participants who are covered exclusively by unfunded plans, even though unfunded plans are not within the universe defined.

† Represents about 30 percent of total Taft–Hartley participants and 47 percent of all other plan participants at the durations studied, a composite figure of 44 percent.

‡ Represents about 7 percent of total Taft–Hartley participants and 24 percent of all other plan participants at the durations studied, a composite figure of 22 percent.

funds required to provide accrued pension benefits in full. (The term "accrued pension benefits" means the pension benefits attributable to service—and, where applicable, compensation earned—prior to the date of study.)

The principal funding summaries are based on a measurement termed "Benefit Security Ratio," a concept developed in an earlier pilot study by one of the authors.[4] The Benefit Secu-

---

[4] Frank L. Griffin, Jr., "Pension Security and Funding Regulation," *The Proceedings of the Conference of Actuaries in Public Practice*, Vol. XIV, pp. 128–38.

rity Ratio (BSR) is the ratio of the value of assets accumulated under a pension plan, to the value of all accrued pension benefits. Thus, on the actuarial basis later described, a BSR of 100 percent (or more) indicates that in event of current plan termination the accrued benefits are fully provided for; a BSR of less than 100 percent indicates that accrued benefits have not yet been fully secured.

[It is necessary to distinguish between (*i*) measurements of the degree of funding under a particular actuarial cost method, and (*ii*) measurements focused on the security of accrued pension benefits at any point of time. For example, the "supplemental cost" (or past-service cost) determined by projected benefit cost methods exceeds the cost of accrued benefits. Therefore, a so-called "funded ratio" (assets divided by "supplemental cost") based on such a method will understate the degree of security enjoyed currently by the employees in question. The "benefit security ratio" (assets divided by cost of accrued benefits) properly reflects current benefit security in event of plan termination.]

Security ratios have been determined both with respect to accrued benefits in total and with respect to accrued benefits that are vested. The latter measure has been termed Vested Benefit Security Ratio (VBSR). A choice between BSR and VBSR obviously will depend upon whether one wishes to measure security of total accrued benefits or of vested benefits only. (The latter measure, it may be noted, is consistent with the attention given to vesting in a recent opinion on pension accounting and in recent proposals by government representatives on the subject of pension funding.) [5]

---

[5] Accounting Principles Board Opinion No. 8, "Accounting for the Cost of Pension Plans." Both the Minimum Pension Provision (para. 17a) and the Disclosure Footnote (para. 46-4) require that consideration be given to the cost of vested benefits for which provision has not already been made.

(*Footnote continues on Page 6.*)

Qualification of the
BSR and VBSR Measurements

Most pension plans include benefits for periods of service rendered prior to inception of the plan and, even subsequent thereto, are subject to periodic improvement of benefits applicable to service before as well as after the date of improvement. The costs associated with benefits for prior service at the time a plan is adopted or amended (usually termed "supplemental costs" or "past-service costs") may be 10, 15, 20 or more times the cost of one year's accrual of benefits. This is a sum so substantial as to make impracticable the achievement of full funding of accrued benefits within a few years of a plan's inception (if indeed ever, when periodic benefit improvements are considered).

Moreover, Internal Revenue Service limitations on pension contributions make it difficult to fund a plan's supplemental costs on a tax-deductible basis in fewer than 12 years (though the use of certain actuarial cost methods in the presence of substantial actuarial gains may sometimes have that effect). Therefore, one would not normally expect to find a plan's Benefit Security Ratio reaching 100 percent in fewer than 10 or 12 years, even if the funding were as rapid as practically possible and even if no increase in past-service benefits had occurred in the interim. Where a plan's supplemental costs are being amortized on a 30-year amortization basis (a basis which is very common, particularly under union negotiated plans), the Benefit Security Ratio might take 30 years to reach 100 percent; and again any interim increase in benefits for prior

---

Stanley S. Surrey's remarks before American Pension Conference, May 11, 1967.

Labor Department Bill, "Pension Benefit Security Act of 1968," introduced by Senator Yarborough as S.3421, May 1968.

service could delay the achievement of a 100 percent Benefit Security Ratio well beyond 30 years.

In assessing the significance of any particular security ratio, therefore, the effective period of past funding (a weighted average considering the number and magnitude of benefit liberalizations over the years) is a better guide than the number of years the plan has been in effect. All plans start from a BSR (and VBSR) of zero and progress upward as the funding of benefits for current and prior service is accomplished; however, each time a benefit liberalization occurs there is a setback both in the security ratio and in the effective period of past funding.

Plans appearing to possess similar characteristics may exhibit a wide variation in security ratios due to other factors which are not always obvious. Among these are the relative extent of past-service benefits being provided, the age distributions of participants, and the existence of bargaining agreements relating to funding. In this study it has not been possible to neutralize or equalize the results for all such factors. As a consequence, it has been necessary to deal in aggregates with respect to certain factors, even though substantial variation among plans is known to be present. This poses the danger of reaching oversimplified conclusions through presumption of identical conditions which do not in fact exist among private pension plans.

A Consistent Basis of Determining Values

Since the actuaries of different consulting firms and insurance companies, if left to their individual judgments, could be expected to derive accrued benefit values on a rather wide range of actuarial assumptions, it was necessary to resolve the problem of providing a single measure of such values which would be consistent with the basis used to value assets. The authors have handled this by having benefit values computed essentially on the basis of the average price available on the open market—that is, at the average of rates offered by leading insurance companies, at the mean valuation date of the study, for purchase of nonparticipating group annuities. To be consistent with this basis of valuing pension liabilities, market values were stipulated for the valuation of assets.

Funding "Benchmarks"

Since a BSR or VBSR "absolute" of 100 percent is not a necessary condition of satisfactory funding progress, the authors have introduced the concept of a funding benchmark related to the effective period of past funding. The concept has been introduced despite the knowledge that an appropriate *uniform* basis of measuring funding progress cannot be postulated due to the existence of widely differing circumstances applicable to different plans. Nonetheless, to provide a means of neutralizing one of the principal variables (funding duration) as well as to illustrate the proportion of plans showing good funding progress, the authors have selected benchmarks which, on theoretical grounds, one might expect a substantial number of plans to follow.

Chart 1–1 illustrates several arbitrary benchmarks. The straight lines as well as curves indicate a few of the possible progressions of BSR's from 0 to 100 percent over varying periods of years. The shape of the two curves shown is consistent with the buildup of security ratios under commonly followed and actuarially acceptable funding procedures, considered in conjunction with typical patterns of employment growth in this country.[6] In order to provide a range of measure-

---

[6] Such curves are characteristic of an initially immature distribution of employees moving gradually toward maturity; mature groups (relatively rare in this country to date) would come closer to being characterized by a straight line

ment both a 30-year straight line (Benchmark 1) and a 40-year curve (Benchmark 2) have been employed in the comparisons of this study. A more complete discussion will be found in Chapter 5 which deals specifically with the question of benchmark comparisons.

CHART 1-1

FUNDING BENCHMARKS
(Illustrative only)

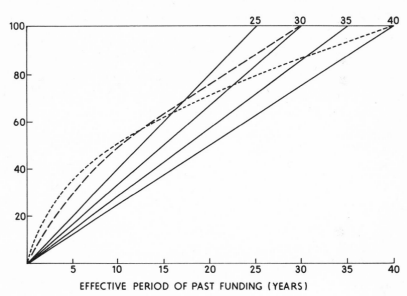

EFFECTIVE PERIOD OF PAST FUNDING (YEARS)

Abbreviated Summary of Findings

Benefit Security Ratios (BSR's) and Vested Benefit Security Ratios (VBSR's) are presented throughout according to effective period of past funding rather than according to the

---

progression of security ratios. This conclusion can be developed from material in Charles L. Trowbridge's paper, "Fundamentals of Pension Funding," *Transactions, Society of Actuaries,* Vol. IV.

total number of years the plan has been in effect. In Chapter 4, these ratios are also displayed according to size of case, scope of coverage (category of employees covered, single or multi-employer plans, collectively bargained or not so bargained), basic type of pension formula, type of funding instrument, classification of vesting (as to liberality), and certain other parameters. Chapter 5 makes similar comparisons in terms of "funding benchmarks."

The general level of security ratios found in this study is apparent from Table 1–2. A rather high plateau appears to have been reached after slightly more than 15 years of effective funding.

Table 1–3 illustrates the *proportion* of plans having security ratios at various levels, according to funding duration. The

TABLE 1–2

SECURITY RATIOS BY EFFECTIVE PERIOD OF PAST FUNDING

Effective Period of Past Funding	Weighted Averages Based on Adjusted Ratios*		Weighted Averages Based on Unadjusted Ratios†	
	BSR	VBSR	BSR	VBSR
Less than 10 years	62.4%	68.3%	63.2%	72.4%
10–14 years	86.6	94.1	108.7	135.5
15–19 years	95.9	98.2	115.6	143.7
20–24 years	94.8	99.2	114.5	143.4
25–29 years	97.4	99.2	112.9	135.8
30 years or more	89.6‡	99.9	103.5‡	144.4
All Periods Combined	84.9%	90.2%	99.9%	123.3%

* Individual plan ratios limited to a maximum of 100 percent, and weighted in the averages by the value of accrued (or vested) benefits. On this basis a BSR or VBSR of 100 percent cannot be reached in any grouping of plans unless *every* plan in the grouping has an individual ratio of 100 percent or more. This measurement is indicative of overall benefit security reached, but not of the ratios achieved by individual plans. This is the basis of displaying *average* security ratios for various groupings of plans in Chapter 4.

† Individual plan ratios allowed to exceed 100 percent and weighted in the averages by the value of accrued (or vested) benefits. This measurement gives some indication of the ratios achieved by individual plans, but not of overall benefit security reached. This is the basis used to construct "duration equalizers" for the *Indices* of Benefit Security shown in Chapter 4.

‡ Excluding one large plan, the average adjusted BSR becomes 99.5 percent and the average *un*adjusted BSR becomes 119.3 percent. After correction for the distortion caused by this one plan the results are in line with the "plateau" observed with respect to plans with effective funding periods in excess of 15 years.

substantial shift in the proportion of plans at different levels of benefit security, as the funding duration increases, is readily apparent.

TABLE 1-3

DISTRIBUTION OF PLANS ACCORDING TO INDIVIDUAL SECURITY RATIOS
AND EFFECTIVE PERIOD OF PAST FUNDING

Effective Period of Past Funding	A. Proportion of Plans Having Benefit Security Ratio (BSR) of:			
	Less than 60%	60–79%	80–99%	100% or More
Less than 10 years	32.3%	25.5%	21.1%	21.1%
10–14 years	13.8	17.3	19.9	49.0
15–19 years	5.8	11.0	16.3	66.9
20–24 years	4.0	9.6	14.2	72.2
25–29 years	5.7	5.7	15.0	73.6
30 years or more	..	7.7	11.5	80.8
All Periods Combined	(12.6%)	(15.1%)	(18.1%)	(54.2%)

Effective Period of Past Funding	B. Proportion of Plans Having Vested Benefit Security Ratio (VBSR) of:			
	Less than 60%	60–79%	80–99%	100% or More
Less than 10 years	16.8%	21.1%	14.9%	47.2%
10–14 years	3.5	8.6	12.3	75.6
15–19 years	2.4	5.2	5.8	86.6
20–24 years	0.6	1.7	7.3	90.4
25–29 years	1.9	1.9	9.5	86.7
30 years or more	..	..	3.8	96.2
All Periods Combined	(4.7%)	(8.1%)	(10.2%)	(77.0%)

Chart 1–2 is a pictorial presentation of the distribution of plans according to BSR, for four classifications by funding duration; this chart also shows the percentage of plans whose BSR's exceed the more stringent of the two benchmarks used in the study. The percentage exceeding this benchmark remains close to 90 percent at all funding durations.

CHART 1–2

Distribution of Plans according to "BSR"
(By Effectve Period of Past Funding)

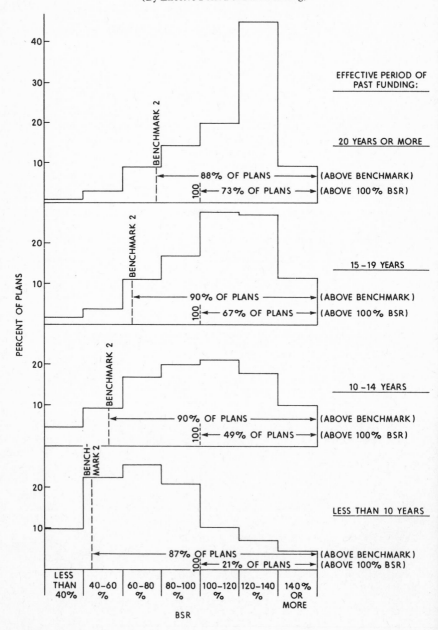

The authors' interpretation of the results of the study is given in Chapter 6. Briefly, the conclusions are:

1. A high degree of benefit security had been achieved by the year 1966 by a vast majority of the plans included in the study. For example, assets were sufficient, on the average, to cover 94.4 percent of all accrued benefits under plans whose effective funding periods were 15 years or more.

2. Considered in relation to the effective period of funding, between 90 and 94 percent of the plans studied had developed benefit security ratios in excess of the two benchmarks of funding progress used by the authors for illustrative purposes.

3. The study furnishes impressive evidence that sound programs of financing have been the rule. While the recent period of rising interest rates has contributed to the favorable results, one may nonetheless conclude that conservative assumptions and cost methods have been employed in the funding of most private pensions.

4. With regard to the extent of vesting found under private pension plans, approximately half of the participants and benefit values in the study were found to be under plans having vesting classified as "early" (essentially after approximately ten years of service). Another one third of the participants and benefit values were found under plans having vesting classified as "intermediate" (less favorable than "early" but essentially prior to satisfaction of early retirement requirements). Overall, 81 percent of the *values* of all accrued benefits were vested. Vesting therefore appears to be at a reasonably advanced stage in its evolution, with liberalizations continuing to occur as other benefit priorities are satisfied.

Chapter 2

Methodology

Any research aimed at meaningful relationships in a complicated area can anticipate problems in methodology. Especially is this true if rather sophisticated data are needed from widely scattered sources, and if the basic units with which one is concerned (here particular pension plans) tend to be heterogeneous. A clear statement of these problems, and of the solution adopted for each, is the main source from which the research design, and hence the usefulness of the study, can be judged. The purpose of this chapter is to discuss the major problems encountered, and to outline the solutions devised. More detail with respect to some of these problems will be found in the "Instructions to Contributors" appearing in the Appendix.

The Universe of Private Pension Plans

The universe of plans toward which this study is directed is the totality of pension plans maintained for employees by private employers in the United States which have some degree of funding in advance of the date that payments fall due. Fixed contribution pension plans are included, as well as more common fixed benefit pension plans.

No attempt has been made to study deferred profit-sharing plans, under which funds are accumulated in part for retirement purposes. Pension plans covering government workers at federal, state, or local levels have not been studied, although many of the questions raised with respect to the funding of private pension plans apply with at least equal force. Nor is this study directed at plans established by government under such legislation as the Social Security and Railroad Retirement Acts which cover workers in private industry. In short, this study is confined to pension plans established by private business firms, unilaterally or through collective bargaining, to provide old-age benefits for their employees.

The so-called "pay-as-you-go" plans, those that make no provision for funding plan benefits until such benefits actually become payable, have been excluded. These plans are by definition unfunded, and for these plans the security ratios with which this study is concerned are therefore known to be zero. Typically, such plans are not "qualified" under the Internal Revenue Code, there being no reason for submitting such plans for qualification. Exclusion of these plans means that the defined universe of private plans is a reasonably close match to the universe of qualified pension plans, though there are some pension plans within the universe that are technically unqualified.

Exclusion of pay-as-you-go plans was based upon practical grounds. From a strictly theoretical point of view, the authors would have preferred to include such plans in the study, or perhaps to have published results for such plans separately, since these plans have unique characteristics related to the purposes of this research. The practical considerations include the lack of contact between these plans and pension actuaries resulting in nonavailability of data, and the lack of government interest because of their nonqualified status. In any event, unfunded plans are not a very important segment of private pensions in toto.

Part I—Identification of
Plans within the Universe

Ideal research design would have involved the obtaining of identifying information on all plans within the defined universe, together with data from which these heterogeneous plans could be classified into their major types. Scientific stratified sampling procedures could then have been expected to produce meaningful results even though the required calculations were performed on a considerably smaller sample than that actually used in this study.

As a practical matter there is no ready source of such identification and classification data. Although statistical data are available from Internal Revenue sources, and although the Labor Department maintains public records of reports under the Welfare and Pension Plans Disclosure Act, there are difficulties in the identification process connected with the exclusion of welfare and profit-sharing plans, as well as difficulties in the classification process resulting from differences between information available and information needed. Since it is apparent that some actuary has a connection with almost every plan within the defined universe, and since an actuary's services necessarily would be required with respect to calculations on any sample of plans selected, actuarial organizations and life insurance companies were chosen as the primary source of identification and classification information. A letter describing the purposes of the project and enlisting cooperation was sent to some 35 actuarial consulting firms and 12 insurance companies thought to be most active in the pension field.

To keep the number of plans within manageable proportions the instructions to contributing firms asked them to exclude plans covering fewer than 25 participants. Although there are many of these small plans and they have some impact on the matters with which this study is concerned, the small number of participants covered by such plans clearly diminishes their relative importance. Contributing firms were also instructed to ignore plans in existence less than 10 years, partly for the purpose of keeping the project within its resources, but also because the many plans established within the last 10 years have not had time to demonstrate the funding patterns into which they may ultimately settle. Funding of less than 10-years' duration is nonetheless represented among the plans included, since in many cases substantial plan additions have been made within the last 10 years.

Twenty-two consulting firms and 11 insurance companies agreed to participate and actually submitted data for Part I, the identification and classification portion of the study. Among those who did not participate were some who had no cases 10 or more years old, others who lacked the personnel to cooperate, and a few who declined for other reasons. Identification and classification data with respect to 3,983 plans were submitted in Part I. It is recognized that these plans include only a portion of the defined universe. Among the missing, in addition to the very small plans and the plans of less than 10-years' duration deliberately excluded, are the following categories:

a) Plans that, for any reason, operate without actuarial help.
b) Plans that obtain actuarial help from the smaller or less active consulting firms or insurance companies whose cooperation was not sought.
c) Plans whose actuarial help comes from consulting firms or insurance companies whose cooperation was sought, but who for one reason or another felt unable to submit the data called for by Part I of this study.

The Part I plans are not necessarily representative of the missing plans with respect to certain of their classification characteristics. At least two broad types of plans are underrepresented: plans funded through individual insurance or annuity contracts, and collectively bargained multiemployer plans.

Insurance company home offices keep records in such a way that the furnishing of information required for the study is extremely difficult on plans financed wholly or in part through the medium of individual life insurance policies. The fact that most individual policy plans tend to cover relatively few participants, however, makes this particular underrepresentation of little significance in the overall picture, especially since plans with fewer than 25 participants were otherwise excluded.

Several actuarial firms particularly active in the multiemployer area were unable to participate in the study. The underrepresentation of collectively bargained multiemployer plans is of more importance because there are a large number of participants covered under such plans.

Selection of Part II Subsample from Part I Plans

The 3,983 plans identified in Part I of this study were still too many to be studied in detail since relatively sophisticated actuarial computations were required. Since the contributing actuarial firms and insurance companies were to be called upon to devote much time and talent to the extensive analyses and calculations required for Part II, a sampling process from the Part I submissions was felt necessary in order not to exceed the resources of the project.

It was felt to be important that the sample include as many as possible of the largest plans because of their importance to the whole. It was also thought that the underrepresentation of collectively bargained multiemployer plans should be corrected to the extent possible. Therefore, for all plans in Part I where the number of participants exceeded 5,000, and for all collectively bargained multiemployer plans regardless of size, the participating firm was requested to furnish Part II data.

For those plans with more than 500 but fewer than 5,000 participants, a 50 percent sample was decided upon, and for those with fewer than 500 participants, a 25 percent sample was used. Actual selection of the sample within the size group was done by throwing punched cards representing the respective plans into a random order deck, then selecting every second card for the 50 percent sample, and every fourth card for the 25 percent sample.

In addition to the intentional reduction in number of plans in Part II, several actuarial firms and insurance companies contributing to Part I were unable to commit the much larger amount of time and talent required by Part II, and the cases that these firms submitted for Part I are entirely missing from Part II. Others contributed most of the cases selected for Part II, but found it impractical for one reason or another to make the analyses and calculations requested on a few of them. Unfortunately, in view of the underrepresentation of Taft–Hartley plans already existing, some of the missing from Part II were of this type.

The method of deliberate selection would seem to involve no particular bias except for the lower proportion of smaller plans, and therefore some degree of bias against those plan characteristics particularly associated with the smaller plans. There may be a slight bias, the direction of which must be regarded as unknown, resulting from the difference between the number of plans selected by the sampling procedure for Part II (1,161) and the number on which Part II data were actually submitted in time for inclusion in the study (1,047).

Obviously, Part II cannot be considered to be a true probability sample of the Part I cases; but neither is Part I a true probability sample of the universe it strives to represent. Thus, only by coincidence would the Part II plans have an identical breakdown by plan characteristics as the larger Part I of which it is a subset. A display of the characteristics of Part II plans appears in Chapter 3 and can be compared with the similar display for Part I plans.

Table 1–1 in the previous chapter compares the numbers of participants in the universe of private plans with those included in Parts I and II. A similar comparison, based on numbers of plans rather than numbers of participants, was attempted; but dependable data do not appear to be available on this point.

Benefits Accrued to Date of Valuation

The principal funding measurement toward which the study aimed is the Benefit Security Ratio (BSR), whose numerator is the value of the assets held by the plan, and whose denominator is the then present value of benefits accrued to date. Another funding measurement illustrated is the Vested Benefit Security Ratio (VBSR) whose denominator includes the present value of only those benefits accrued to date that are vested—i.e., are not contingent upon continued employment.

The benefit formulas for many pension plans clearly allocate the eventual pension benefit for any particular employee according to his years of employment. Where this is the case, the benefit accrued to date at any point in time is the pension (and any corollary benefits that attach themselves thereto) attributable to employment prior to that date.

The problem of methodology involved here is that not all benefit formulas relate the ultimate pension benefit to years of service. Others may in general do so but impose maximum or minimum pensions not directly related to service. Still others give no credit for service in excess of some stated number of years (such as 25), and it is not always clear, for a man who is to have 35 years of service at retirement, whether the ten missing credits are to be viewed as the first 10, the last 10, or as 10 distributed proportionately between past and future years.

The instructions for Part II to be found in the Appendix indicate how this matter of definition of benefits accrued to date was resolved. In general, the exact determination was left to the actuarial organization making the calculation, since it is in the best position to know the background of the design of the benefit formula, and how it is explained to employees. Clues can often be found in the plan's provisions with respect to early retirement or vested withdrawal. Where there was no good reason to make any choice except a completely arbitrary one, a rule based on proportionality—equal weight to all years of service—was specified. For final average salary plans the actuarial organizations were permitted to calculate benefits accrued to date on the basis of salary as of date of valuation, even though this may overstate the amount under the plan's provisions.

Present Value of Accrued Benefits

Having determined for each participant his pension benefits accrued to date, an actuary can then calculate the value, as of a particular moment of time, of these future benefits. Techniques for converting a series of future payments into a single-sum present value are among the tools of every qualified pension actuary. There is no reason to describe such techniques here, except to say that they involve assumptions as to future rates of investment earnings and probabilities of survival. The later the date that a future payment becomes due, the less its value today, both because of the effect of compound interest, and because the actual payment is contingent on the member's living to receive it. Employee withdrawal rates are not a factor in the calculation of present values in this study, though they often are used in similar calculations performed for different purposes.

The problem of methodology that shows up here is that no two actuaries, except by coincidence, would select the same assumptions as to interest and mortality. Interest earnings vary over time and also with the type of investment. Mortality rates also vary over time, but in addition are a function of age, sex, state of present health, and to a lesser extent socioeconomic class, geographical location, and occupation.

Since the choice of assumptions exerts considerable leverage on the present value of benefits accrued to date, and hence on the denominators of both the BSR and the VBSR, it was felt necessary to specify the actuarial assumptions so that all calculations would be on a comparable and reasonably realistic basis.

The authors of this monograph, who directed the actuarial phases of this project, make no claim to any better view of future interest rates or future mortality experience than any other actuaries. They were therefore reluctant to impose their judgment on others, and did not, in fact, do so. Instead, they asked 12 life insurance companies in March, 1966, to quote nonparticipating group rates at which they would be willing to sell deferred and immediate pension benefits. The rates obtained presumably contained provision for the expenses of the company and for any profit or contingency reserve needed in view of the risk undertaken. In this sense, the rates obtained may be considered to be slightly conservative, meaning that they slightly overstate the benefit values and consequently understate the benefit security ratios.

The authors then constructed a set of actuarial assumptions, which have no other significance than the fact that they can be shown to produce results in the middle of the range established by the life insurance company rates referred to above. The authors view the tables specified in the Instructions as representative of the average market price at which nonparticipating group annuities could be bought as of March, 1966.

There is one noteworthy matter in connection with the establishment of the tables used in valuing the benefits accrued to date. The tables were constructed to produce March, 1966, market rates. Interest yields at which long-term investments could be bought in March, 1966, were higher than at many times in the past even though lower than has been obtained at most times since (up to the date of writing). To a major degree, the insurance company quotations reflect the rates at which money could be invested in the long-term market at that particular time. This has an important bearing when assets are to be compared with present values of benefits accrued to date.

Value of Assets

The determination of the dollar value of the asset figure, the numerator of the ratios under consideration, also involves some important problems. There can be no asset figure which would enjoy general acceptance for the purpose to which it is being put. In particular, problems revolve around the question of book value versus market value, and the details involved in the calculation of each.

Book Value. Most pension funds and insurance companies compute a book value of assets. Book value is essentially based on the long look, and the underlying assumptlon that disposal of the asset before its date of maturity is unlikely.

For debt investment, typically bonds or mortgages, the book value is usually the face amount of the outstanding debt, if the original purchase of the investment was at par. If not, the original premium or discount is often amortized over the period of the indebtedness.

The book value can be viewed as the present value of future payments due, using the original yield rate as the rate of capitalization. For common stocks, real estate, or other forms of equity investment the book value is likely to be cost, the amount originally invested; although where the time since purchase is long, and the difference between market value and original cost is great, the book values of equity investment may have been adjusted toward market.

Book value tends to be relatively stable, and is readily computed. It has little meaning with respect to common stocks, however; and for the purposes of this study the book value has theoretical difficulties in that it values debt securities on an original yield basis, while the present values of accrued benefits (with which the value of the assets is being compared) are, in effect, being valued on the basis of interest yields available on representative current new investments of life insurance companies. Although the Instructions ask for book value as well as market value, the latter was actually used in the calculation of the benefit security ratios.

Market Value. By "market value" is meant the dollars for which a particular investment could be exchanged on a given date in a free market bringing together a willing buyer and a willing seller.

Some securities are readily marketable, and value quotations for such securities can be obtained at almost any time through organized exchanges, or through investment banking firms. Good examples of securities with easily determinable market values are common stocks and publicly offered bonds.

Other assets commonly held by pension plans or insurance companies have much less marketability, and there is no source of meaningful price quotations. Examples of these hard-to-value types of investments are real estate mortgages, real estate, and privately placed bonds or debentures.

A characteristic of market value that must be noted is its volatility, with the result that values are very sensitive to the particular point in the time scale at which the inventory is taken. The value of common stock, particularly, is subject to the vagaries of the market place, and its erratic behavior is well known. It is perhaps not quite so universally appreciated that the market value of debt instruments also fluctuates rather widely, partly because the probability of default may vary over time, but more importantly because of swings in the interest rates at which long-term funds can be invested. A well-secured bond bearing a 3½ percent coupon rate and a maturity 25 years hence is worth $1,000 when investors are willing to invest long-term funds at 3½ percent; but is worth only $730 when the money market has changed to a point that long-term investors obtain 5½ percent for a similar degree of risk.

Since long-term interest rates were generally increasing during the period when this study was being conducted, market values of debt instruments were moving downward.

Despite the volatility of market value, and despite the difficulty of determining market value for the less marketable types of investments, the Instructions called for market value as the primary measure of assets. Consulting firms working with trust fund plans had relatively little difficulty in furnishing market value, since pension trusts usually invest in marketable securities and trustees commonly furnish both market and book values as a matter of routine reporting of pension plan assets. Insurance companies furnished approximations to market value, based in most cases on their investment year methods of interest allocation. These have become the rule rather than the exception among life insurance companies active in the group pension field. For such companies the principle of the adjustment from book value to market value can be illustrated by the following oversimplified formula:

$$\frac{\text{Market value}}{\text{Book value}} = 1 - K(i - i')$$

where i = the rate of interest on current investment

i' = the average yield rate on the particular mix of investment years which make up the pension assets for the plan in question.

K is a multiplier, usually in the general range from 5 to 10, derived from rates of reinvestment.

If, for example, K were 7, i were 6 percent, and i' were 5 percent, market value would be computed as 93 percent of book value.

In any event, the investigators relied on the actuarial firm reporting to furnish market values, either exactly or approximately. In a very few cases, where market values were not furnished, approximations were made by the authors.

The particular virtue of market value as a measure of assets is that with respect to debt investment the market value reflects the then current rate of return on long-term investment. Since the denominators of the benefit security ratios are also computed on a market value basis, which reflects the then current situation as to yields obtainable on fixed income securities in the long-term market, it is important in computing the ratios that both market values be calculated at nearly the same point in time.

Timing Considerations

Since the market survey on which the rates for present value purposes were based was undertaken in March, 1966, one approach to the minimization of timing problems would have been the calculation of assets values for all plans as of

March, 1966. This approach was discarded for both theoretical and practical reasons. The use of a single date puts too much dependence upon the level of the stock market on that date, even if the single date is particularly well chosen. It was felt that some stock market averaging could be incorporated, and at the same time the practical difficulties in the Part II calculations could be much reduced, if the date as of which the assets (and liabilities) were valued was left to the convenience of the actuarial firm or insurance company involved. As a result, the time at which assets were actually valued were plan anniversaries in 1965, 1966, or 1967. The distribution of these plan anniversaries is shown later (Table 3–14), and the mean date, weighted by the denominator of the ratios under study, is about April 1, 1966. This mean date is close to the March, 1966, annuity-rate survey date, which tends to minimize problems of interpretation. There are nonetheless implications with respect to timing differences, the discussion of which will be found in Chapter 6.

Effective Period of Past Funding

The BSR's and VBSR's to which this study is directed indicate the degree of funding that a plan has accomplished at any point of time. Whether a particular BSR or VBSR can be viewed as high or low depends on the size of the ratio itself, but also clearly depends upon how long the plan has been in the funding process.

The plans in this study have all been in effect for 10 or more years, and thus by any standard should have made some progress with respect to the benefit security ratios. On the other hand, plans are not homogeneous with respect to the time they have been in effect, and perhaps even more important, with respect to the timing of benefit liberalizations.

It has been the history of the private pension movement

that many of the older plans have had one or more upward adjustments in formulas for determining pension benefits. Such adjustments have not only occurred frequently in recent years, but some of them have been very substantial. Any increase in benefits is essentially the same for funding purposes as if a new plan for the increased benefit were then being started.

As a classification parameter, the authors have computed for each case in the Part II study an "effective period of past funding," based on an inquiry in the Part II Instructions as to the timing and amount of any increases in plan benefits within the most recent 10 years. The principle behind this effective period of past funding can be shown by a simple example. If a plan has been in existence for 15 years, but had a 100 percent increase in benefits 5 years ago, the weighted years of funding is 10 years (15 years weighted ½, 5 years weighted ½).

For cases without significant change in benefit formula during the most recent 10 years, the effective period of past funding becomes the years the plan has been in effect developed from Part I information.

Since all benefit liberalizations which occurred more than 10 years ago or which individually were less than 10 percent in amount are ignored, the effective period of past funding is somewhat overstated, and the resulting displays should be interpreted accordingly.

Chapter 3

Characteristics of the Plans Studied

The sample of private pension plans which constitutes Part I of this study includes 3,983 plans covering 9,114,000 participants. The Part II subsample reduced the number of plans to 1,047 and the participants to 4,562,000. The more than proportional representation of the large plans in the subsample is apparent. Part I includes about 44 percent of the total participants under funded private plans in effect at least 10 years, whereas Part II represents about 22 percent.

From Part I Reports

Table 3–1 displays the distribution of Part I and Part II plans by years each plan has been in effect. Plans in effect less than 10 years do not appear in either Part I or Part II. The average duration of plans included is about 17 years for both the Part I sample and the Part II subsample, or 19 years when weighted by numbers of participants. The years a plan has been in effect should not be confused with the effective period of past funding described in Chapter 2 and illustrated later in this chapter.

Table 3–2 shows the characteristics of both the Part I sample and the Part II subsample by number of plan participants. In both cases plans of 100 but fewer than 500 participants are the most numerous; but within the cases of 25,000

TABLE 3-1

DISTRIBUTION BY YEARS PLAN IN EFFECT

Years Plan in Effect	Part I—Sample				Part II—Subsample			
	Number of Plans	%	Thousands of Participants	%	Number of Plans	%	Thousands of Participants	%
10–14 years	1,686	42.3	2,416	26.5	423	40.3	1,164	25.5
15–19 years	1,070	26.9	2,905	31.9	300	28.7	1,865	40.9
20–24 years	783	19.7	1,365	15.0	215	20.5	762	16.7
25–29 years	291	7.3	1,029	11.3	76	7.3	411	9.0
30 years or more	153	3.8	1,399	15.3	33	3.2	360	7.9
Total	3,983	100.0	9,114	100.0	1,047	100.0	4,562	100.0

Average

By plans .... 16.9 years   17.0 years

By participants .... 19.4 years   18.7 years

TABLE 3-2

DISTRIBUTION BY NUMBER OF PARTICIPANTS

Number of Participants in Plan	Part I—Sample			Part II—Subsample			
	Number of Plans	%	Thousands of Participants	%	Number of Plans	%	Thousands of Participants	%
25 but fewer than 100	1,061	26.6	74	0.8	184	17.6	13	0.3
100 but fewer than 500	1,560	39.2	468	5.2	307	29.3	92	2.0
500 but fewer than 1,000	525	13.2	394	4.3	193	18.4	145	3.2
1,000 but fewer than 5,000 ...	588	14.7	1,588	17.4	227	21.7	613	13.4
5,000 but fewer than 25,000 ...	198	5.0	2,614	28.7	103	9.8	1,360	29.8
25,000 or more	51	1.3	3,976	43.6	33	3.2	2,339	51.3
Total	3,983	100.0	9,114	100.0	1,047	100.0	4,562	100.0

Average number of
participants per plan 2,288   4,357

participants or more are 44 percent of the total participants in Part I and 51 percent of the total in Part II. The average number of participants per Part I plan is 2,288, but due to including as many of the large plans as possible in Part II, the average number of participants per Part II plan is 4,357.

Table 3–3 shows, for each of Part I and Part II, four different distributions related to coverage. These are:

1. Hourly employees only v. salaried employees only v. plans covering all employees.
2. Single employer plans v. multiemployer.
3. Bargained plans v. nonbargained.
4. Multiemployer bargained plans v. all others.

In each category the number of participants per plan, while not specifically shown in Table 3–3, can easily be ascertained by dividing thousands of participants by number of plans. Part I plans covering hourly employees only are larger on the average than those covering salaried or all employees; similarly, multiemployer plans are larger than single employer, and bargained plans are larger than nonbargained. In Part II similar relationships hold, with the single exception that in the subsample single employer plans are larger on the average than multiemployer plans.

Table 3–4 categorizes the plans within the study by type of pension formula. The relatively small number of defined contribution plans of the cents-per-hour type is probably accounted for by the fact that most plans negotiated on a cents-per-hour basis are eventually redefined in fixed benefit form, and so appear in the study. The service-related defined benefit plans dominate, and the three classifications within this dominant group are not too different in number of participants, particularly in Part II.

Table 3–5 categorizes the plans within the study by fund-

TABLE 3-3

DISTRIBUTION BY COVERAGE

Coverage	Part I—Sample				Part II—Subsample			
	Number of Plans	%	Thousands of Participants	%	Number of Plans	%	Thousands of Participants	%
Hourly employees only	859	21.6	2,866	31.4	275	26.3	1,690	37.1
Salaried employees only	936	23.5	1,383	15.2	256	24.4	782	17.1
All employees	2,188	54.9	4,865	53.4	516	49.3	2,090	45.8
Total	3,983	100.0	9,114	100.0	1,047	100.0	4,562	100.0
Single employer	3,834	96.3	7,866	86.3	977	93.3	4,303	94.3
Multiemployer	149	3.7	1,248	13.7	70	6.7	259	5.7
Total	3,983	100.0	9,114	100.0	1,047	100.0	4,562	100.0
Bargained	896	22.5	3,772	41.4	305	29.1	2,398	52.6
Not bargained	3,087	77.5	5,342	58.6	742	70.9	2,164	47.4
Total	3,983	100.0	9,114	100.0	1,047	100.0	4,562	100.0
Multiemployer and bargained	97	2.4	872	9.6	38	3.6	229	5.0
All others	3,886	97.6	8,242	90.4	1,009	96.4	4,333	95.0
Total	3,983	100.0	9,114	100.0	1,047	100.0	4,562	100.0

TABLE 3-4

Distribution by Type of Pension Formula

Type of Formula	Part I—Sample				Part II—Subsample			
	Number of Plans	%	Thousands of Participants	%	Number of Plans	%	Thousands of Participants	%
Defined contribution plans								
% of compensation	187	4.7	179	2.0	44	4.2	56	1.2
¢ per hour	33	0.8	411	4.5	12	1.2	14	0.3
Defined benefit plans								
Service-related								
% of final compensation ...	993	24.9	2,304	25.3	325	31.0	1,440	31.6
% of career compensation ..	1,628	40.9	3,138	34.4	360	34.4	1,402	30.7
Flat $ amount	785	19.7	2,429	26.7	240	22.9	1,490	32.7
Not service-related								
% of compensation	294	7.4	515	5.6	48	4.6	79	1.7
Flat $ benefit	63	1.6	138	1.5	18	1.7	81	1.8
Total	3,983	100.0	9,114	100.0	1,047	100.0	4,562	100.0

TABLE 3-5

DISTRIBUTION BY FUNDING INSTRUMENT

Funding Instrument	Part I—Sample				Part II—Subsample			
	Number of Plans	%	Thousands of Participants	%	Number of Plans	%	Thousands of Participants	%
I. Individually allocated instruments								
A. Individual policies or group permanent	213	5.4	63	0.7	38	3.6	20	0.4
B. Group deferred annuity	740	18.6	768	8.4	146	13.9	226	5.0
II. Unallocated instruments								
C. Trust fund	1,885	47.3	5,572	61.1	594	56.8	3,452	75.7
D. Deposit administration or IPG	571	14.3	544	6.0	135	12.9	148	3.2
E. C with D	251	6.3	1,477	16.2	67	6.4	341	7.5
III. Allocated and unallocated combinations								
F. A or B with C, D, or E	323	8.1	690	7.6	67	6.4	375	8.2
Total	3,983	100.0	9,114	100.0	1,047	100.0	4,562	100.0

ing instrument. Six general categories of funding instrument (A, B, C, D, E, and F) are shown. These six are grouped into three larger classifications (I, II, and III). Particularly in this table is it evident that the Part I sample is not representative of the universe of all plans. The A category is clearly underrepresented as to number of plans, but, since such funding instruments typically cover smaller groups of participants, it is underrepresented to a considerably lesser degree in terms of participants covered. Again the number of participants per plan for any funding instrument can be computed from the data shown, and those funding instruments particularly associated with the larger plans (e.g., trust fund) have a higher percentage of participants than of number of plans.

Table 3–6 categorizes the answers to questions with respect to funding practice. More than 99 percent of the plans in both Parts I and II were reported as meeting normal costs in full. Approximately 90 percent were reported as either fully funded or as funding supplemental costs in uniform or nonuniform annual installments. (It should again be recognized that pay-as-you-go plans are not included in the study.) It should also be noted that a report on current funding practices does not necessarily indicate the nature of past funding practices, which are perhaps more closely related to the funding questions under study.

The six general areas to which Tables 3–1 to 3–6 are directed summarize Part I and Part II data according to the classifications found on the Part I reporting form. In addition to these six one-dimensional displays, it is possible to display numbers of plans and numbers of participants by any of the 15 two-dimensional combinations of the six basic classification areas. Because such two-way classifications are of limited interest, only one such classification is shown. Table 3–7 is a two-dimensional display of Part II data only by distribution by

TABLE 3-6

DISTRIBUTION BY CURRENT FUNDING PRACTICE

Current Funding Practice	Part I—Sample				Part II—Subsample			
	Number of Plans	%	Thousands of Participants	%	Number of Plans	%	Thousands of Participants	%
Normal cost								
Being met in full	3,963	99.5	9,071	99.5	1,040	99.3	4,558	99.9
Not being met in full	20	0.5	43	0.5	7	0.7	4	0.1
Total	3,983	100.0	9,114	100.0	1,047	100.0	4,562	100.0
Supplemental cost								
Already fully funded*	318	8.0	671	7.4	88	8.4	355	7.8
Funded regularly in relatively uniform installments†	2,719	68.3	5,471	60.0	674	64.4	2,896	63.5
Funded irregularly in nonuniform installments	571	14.3	1,617	17.7	168	16.0	870	19.1
Payment of interest only	279	7.0	848	9.3	94	9.0	395	8.6
Terminal funding	24	0.6	69	0.8	2	0.2	3	0.1
Other	72	1.8	438	4.8	21	2.0	43	0.9
Total	3,983	100.0	9,114	100.0	1,047	100.0	4,562	100.0

* According to cost method in use. A much larger number of plans have accrued benefits fully funded (i.e., BSR of at least 100 percent).
† Including those reported as using cost methods that do not employ the supplemental cost concept, but which typically fund in relatively uniform installments.

TABLE 3-7

DISTRIBUTION OF PART II SUBSAMPLE BY COVERAGE AND FUNDING INSTRUMENT

	Funding Instrument											
	Class I Allocated				Class II Unallocated				Class III Combinations Allocated and Unallocated			
Coverage	Number of Plans	%	Thousands of Participants	%	Number of Plans	%	Thousands of Participants	%	Number of Plans	%	Thousands of Participants	%
Hourly employees only	7	3.8	5	2.0	265	33.3	1,683	42.7	3	4.5	1	0.3
Salaried employees only	39	21.2	101	41.1	201	25.3	496	12.6	16	23.9	186	49.6
All employees	138	75.0	140	56.9	330	41.4	1,762	44.7	48	71.6	188	50.1
Total	184	100.0	246	100.0	796	100.0	3,941	100.0	67	100.0	375	100.0
Single employer	172	93.5	239	97.2	740	93.0	3,690	93.6	65	97.0	374	99.7
Multiemployer	12	6.5	7	2.8	56	7.0	251	6.4	2	3.0	1	0.3
Total	184	100.0	246	100.0	796	100.0	3,941	100.0	67	100.0	375	100.0
Bargained	12	6.5	53	21.5	286	35.9	2,296	58.2	7	10.4	49	13.1
Not bargained	172	93.5	193	78.5	510	64.1	1,647	41.8	60	89.6	326	86.9
Total	184	100.0	246	100.0	796	100.0	3,941	100.0	67	100.0	375	100.0
Multiemployer and bargained	1	0.5	...	...	37	4.6	229	5.8	...	...	...	...
All other	183	99.5	246	100.0	759	95.4	3,712	94.2	67	100.0	375	100.0
Total	184	100.0	246	100.0	796	100.0	3,941	100.0	67	100.0	375	100.0

coverage combined with distribution by funding instrument. Essentially it is a combination of data summarized in Tables 3–3 and 3–5. The authors' purpose in including this single two-dimensional display is to illustrate that the six primary classification areas cannot be assumed to be independent. In Table 3–7 we find a markedly different distribution by coverage for Class II funding instruments than for Classes I or III. Similarly there is a markedly different distribution by funding instrument for hourly employees or for bargained plans than for salaried employees and nonbargained plans. Such lack of independence causes some problems of interpretation, to be commented upon later.

From Part II Reports

Part II reports yielded some important additional information as to plan characteristics with respect to those 1,047 plans submitted for Part II. Particularly related to the secondary purpose of this inquiry are data with respect to vesting.

Table 3–8 shows the distribution of Part II plans by vesting provisions. The vesting provisions encountered were classified as early, intermediate or late. If full vesting occurs after 10 or fewer years of service, vesting was classified as early; if after 11 to 20 years, the classification was intermediate; if full vesting is delayed beyond 20 years, vesting was considered to be late. The detailed rules for classification where age, rather than service, is the vesting requirement, or where vesting is gradual, will be found on Table 3–8. Table 3–8 shows a higher percentage in the early classification (and a lower percentage in the late classification) by thousands of participants than it does by number of plans. This indicates a tendency for the larger plans to have earlier vesting.

TABLE 3–8

DISTRIBUTION BY VESTING CLASSIFICATION

Vesting Classification	Plans		Thousands of Participants	
	No.	%	No.	%
Early	286	27.3	2,156	47.3
Intermediate	439	41.9	1,542	33.8
Late	322	30.8	864	18.9
Total	1,047	100.0	4,562	100.0

Early vesting —Full vesting after 10 (or fewer) years of service.

Intermediate vesting—Full vesting after 11 to 20 years of service.

Late vesting —Full vesting after 21 years or more of service.

Where vesting is stated in terms of age rather than service, the age requirement minus 30 is substituted for the service requirement.

Where *both* service and age requirements must be met, the longer of the two is used.

Where *either* of two alternate vesting requirements is specified, the shorter is assumed.

Where vesting occurs gradually over a period of time, vesting is treated as if equivalent to full vesting at the midpoint of the period.

Table 3–9 shows for each vesting classification and for the total of Part II plans, the value of vested accrued benefits as a percentage of the value of all accrued benefits. Table 3–10 indicates the proportion of the value of all accrued benefits attributable to retired lives, vested terminations, active vested employees, and the active nonvested. With respect to data shown in Tables 3–9 and 3–10, it should be emphasized that the percentages shown are with respect to the value of benefits, not with respect to the amount of benefits or the number of participants. Although 81.0 percent of the values of accrued benefits are vested, both the percent of benefits which are vested and the percent of participants currently having fully vested benefits would be lower. The design of the study does not permit the calculation of the latter.

TABLE 3–9

VALUE OF VESTED BENEFITS AS A PERCENT OF ALL ACCRUED BENEFITS

Vesting *Classification*	*Millions of Dollars* *Value of Accrued Benefits*		*% Vested*
	Vested	*All*	
Early	9,249	10,093	91.6
Intermediate	6,556	7,866	83.3
Late	2,180	4,252	51.3
Total	17,985	22,211	81.0

TABLE 3–10

VALUE OF VESTED BENEFITS BY PARTICIPANT CLASSIFICATION

Participant *Classification*	*Millions of Dollars* *Value of Accrued Benefits*	*% of Total*
Vested		
Retired	5,906	26.6
Terminated but not retired	311	1.4
Active	11,768	53.0
Nonvested		
Active	4,226	19.0
Total	22,211	100.0

Table 3–11 shows the distribution of Part II plans by "effective period of past funding," a classification parameter defined in Chapter 2, related to the number of years that the plan has been in effect, but adjusted for the amount and timing of benefit increases. This average is 15 years by plans, one-half year more when weighted by number of participants. The reader may find a comparison between Tables 3–1 and 3–11 worthwhile.

Table 3–12 shows the distribution of Part II plans by number of benefit increases reported within the most recent 10 years and the amount of such increases. This table is therefore

TABLE 3–11

DISTRIBUTION OF PART II SUBSAMPLE BY EFFECTIVE PERIOD OF PAST FUNDING

Effective Period of Past Funding	Number of Plans	%	Thousands of Participants	%	Millions of Dollars Value of Accrued Benefits	%
Less than 10 years	161	15.3	1,240	27.2	5,060	22.8
10–14 years	422	40.3	1,473	32.3	6,317	28.4
15–19 years	209	20.0	656	14.4	3,160	14.2
20–24 years	176	16.8	569	12.5	2,695	12.1
25–29 years	53	5.1	299	6.5	2,255	10.2
30 years or more	26	2.5	325	7.1	2,724	12.3
Total	1,047	100.0	4,562	100.0	22,211	100.0

Average
By plans...........15.1 years
By participants.....15.6 years

TABLE 3–12

DISTRIBUTION OF PART II SUBSAMPLE BY NUMBER AND
AMOUNT OF BENEFIT INCREASES WITHIN MOST RECENT 10 YEARS

	Number of Plans	%	Thousands of Participants	%
Number of benefit increases (of 10% or more)				
0	509	48.6	1,224	26.8
1	306	29.2	1,242	27.2
2	140	13.4	902	19.8
3	73	7.0	1,127	24.7
4 or more	19	1.8	67	1.5
Total	1,047	100.0	4,562	100.0
Average number				
By plans...........0.8				
By participants.....1.5				
Amount of benefit increase (in total)				
0–9%	509	48.6	1,224	26.8
10–49%	324	30.9	1,901	41.7
50–99%	141	13.5	691	15.1
100% or more	73	7.0	746	16.4
Total	1,047	100.0	4,562	100.0

Average amount
By plan 29.0%
By participants.....50.8%

the explanation of the difference between Tables 3–1 and 3–11. A breakdown of this information according to type of funding instrument shows a significant difference in the number and extent of benefit liberalizations under allocated and unallocated instruments. Plans in the latter category experienced approximately eight times as great an increase in benefits during the most recent 10 years as plans in the former category.

Table 3–13 shows the distribution of Part II plans by percentage of assets invested in equities. The tendency for the larger plans to have a higher proportion invested in equities is apparent.

TABLE 3–13

DISTRIBUTION OF PART II SUBSAMPLE BY PERCENT INVESTED IN EQUITIES

Percentage of Assets Invested in Equities	Number of Plans	%	Millions of Assets	%
0	210	20.1	3,041	13.7
1–10	211	20.1	1,908	8.6
11–25	44	4.2	861	3.9
26–40	120	11.5	3,073	13.9
41–55	279	26.6	3,771	17.0
56–70	161	15.4	9,166	41.3
71–85	18	1.7	238	1.1
86–100	4	0.4	121	0.5
Total 1,047		100.0	22,179	100.0

Average percentage
  By plan......30.1%
  By assets.....41.6%

Table 3–14 shows the distribution of Part II plans by date as of which Part II calculations were performed, a matter of some significance which will be commented upon in Chapter 6. Ninety-one percent of the plans and 89 percent of the accrued benefit values are concentrated at valuation dates falling within the six quarters from October 1, 1965 through March 31, 1967.

TABLE 3–14

DISTRIBUTION OF PART II SUBSAMPLE BY DATE OF CALCULATION

Date of Calculation	Number of Plans	%	Millions of Dollars Value of Accrued Benefits	%
Before 1965	18	1.7	114	0.5
1965 1st quarter	13	1.2	1,687	7.6
2nd quarter	3	0.3	12	0.1
3rd quarter	9	0.9	345	1.6
4th quarter	19	1.8	3,140	14.1
1966 1st quarter	189	18.1	7,043	31.7
2nd quarter	39	3.7	215	1.0
3rd quarter	112	10.7	1,270	5.7
4th quarter	114	10.9	1,106	5.0
1967 1st quarter	480	45.8	6,964	31.3
2nd quarter	21	2.0	229	1.0
3rd quarter	25	2.4	82	0.4
4th quarter	5	0.5	4	...
Total	1,047	100.0	22,211	100.0

Average date
  By plans, September, 1966
  By value of accrued benefits, April, 1966

Chapter 4

Study Results in Terms of Benefit Security

This chapter presents the results of detailed actuarial calculations which measure the degree of benefit security existing under the 1,047 plans included in Part II of the study. Benefit security under any particular plan is measured by the extent to which the value of all pensions attributable to service to the valuation date is matched by the value of assets already accumulated as of that date. This may therefore be interpreted as a measure of the ability of a plan to provide accrued benefits in full in the event it were to terminate on the valuation date.

The ratio of the value of assets to the value of all accrued benefits is the "Benefit Security Ratio" (BSR). The "Vested Benefit Security Ratio" (VBSR) is comparable in every way except that it relates only to the value of those accrued benefits that are *vested*. In order to obtain both types of security ratio, total accrued benefits as well as vested accrued benefits were computed, and an actuarial valuation made to obtain the value of such accrued benefits for comparison with asset values.

Overall, for the 1,047 plans, aggregate asset values of $22.2 billions (market values) compare with a value of accrued benefits also totalling $22.2 billions, and with a total

45

value of *vested* accrued benefits of $18.0 billions.[1] Aggregate figures do not provide meaningful benefit security indicators in themselves, however, not only because variations according to duration of funding and other parameters are not reflected, but also because an excess of assets over accrued benefit values for one plan cannot properly be offset against an excess of accrued benefit values over assets for another.

In order to obtain results in various meaningful ways, both unadjusted and adjusted security ratios were computed for each plan. The unadjusted ratio for any plan consists simply of the ratio of the value of its assets to the value of its accrued benefits (which in many cases will run in excess of 100 percent), whereas the adjusted ratio is limited to a maximum of 100 percent for any plan.

Although unadjusted ratios are not suitable benefit security indicators when plans are grouped for an average, they are useful in displaying distributions of plans according to security ratio, as well as in identifying the benefit security characteristics of individual plans and the true spread between plans.

In obtaining averages for groups of plans, such as are displayed in Tables 4–2 and subsequent, the adjusted ratio has universally been used in order to avoid overstatement arising from what in effect would be a subsidization of an underfunded plan by an overfunded plan. On this basis a BSR or VBSR of 100 percent cannot be reached in any grouping of plans unless *every* plan in the grouping has an individual ratio of 100 percent or more.

Table 4–1 sets forth a *distribution* of plans according to their individual unadjusted security ratios, for all periods of

---

[1] The close correspondence between the first two of these dollar values— which differ by less than $32 million—is of course accidental.

past funding combined. Approximately 54 percent of the plans (having 48 percent of the participants and 54 percent of the accrued benefit values) have already reached a Benefit Security Ratio of 100 percent or more. Approximately 77 percent of the plans (having 64 percent of the participants and 66 percent of the *vested* benefit values) have already reached a Vested Benefit Security Ratio of 100 percent or more.

It is apparent that the proportion of plans having security ratios at or above a given level will depend on the period funding has been under way. Since over half of the plans included in these statistics (covering well over half of the participants) have effective periods of past funding of less than 15 years, the frequency with which security ratios of 100 percent or more are found is quite significant. Moreover, when separate distributions are obtained for different funding durations (as exhibited in Table 1–3 of Chapter 1) another significant item emerges. The proportion of plans having a BSR of less than 80 percent drops by about seven eighths as the effective period of past funding moves from less than 10 years to 30 years or more (a funding interval of approximately 25 years), while over the same funding interval the proportion of plans having a BSR of 100 percent or more increases four times.

Charts 4–1 and 4–2 further illustrate the effect of funding duration on the proportion of plans having security ratios at or above a given level.

These charts provide a simple means of determining the proportion of plans which exceed a specified security ratio, or the converse, according to funding duration category.

TABLE 4-1

DISTRIBUTION OF PLANS ACCORDING TO UNADJUSTED SECURITY RATIOS,
WITHOUT REGARD TO FUNDING DURATION,* AND NUMBERS OF PARTICIPANTS COVERED THEREUNDER

Unadjusted Security Ratios	Distribution of Plans			Participants Covered under Such Plans		
	Number of Plans	% of Total	% at or above Indicated BSR Group	Thousands of Participants	% of Total	% at or above Indicated BSR Group
TOTAL ACCRUED BENEFITS						
Plan BSR						
Less than 40%	41	3.9%	100.0%	150	3.3%	100.0%
40–59%	91	8.7	96.1	315	6.9	96.7
60–79%	158	15.1	87.4	1,337	29.3	89.8
80–99%	189	18.1	72.3	558	12.2	60.5
100–119%	214	20.4	54.2	1,056	23.1	48.3
120–139%	259	24.7	33.8	610	13.4	25.2
140–159%	55	5.3	9.1	177	3.9	11.8
160% or more	40	3.8	3.8	359	7.9	7.9
All	1,047	100.0%		4,562	100.0%	
VESTED ACCRUED BENEFITS ONLY						
Plan VBSR						
Less than 40%	11	1.1%	100.0%	49	1.1%	100.0%
40–59%	38	3.6	98.9	107	2.3	98.9
60–79%	85	8.1	95.3	1,035	22.7	96.6
80–99%	107	10.2	87.2	459	10.1	73.9
100–119%	124	11.9	77.0	456	10.0	63.8
120–139%	178	17.0	65.1	806	17.7	53.8
140–159%	110	10.5	48.1	297	6.5	36.1
160% or more	394	37.6	37.6	1,353	29.6	29.6
All	1,047	100.0%		4,562	100.0%	

* *Effective period of past funding, which for the plans in the study varies from 4 to 50 years.*

CHART 4–1

<small>PERCENTAGE OF PLANS WITH BSR AT INDICATED LEVEL OR HIGHER</small>
(Vertical Scale)

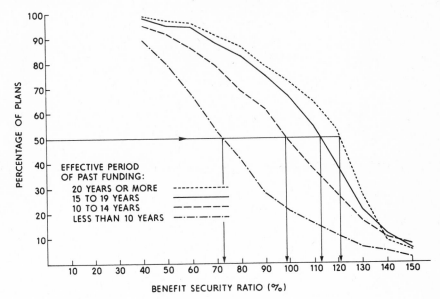

BENEFIT SECURITY RATIO (%)

<small>ILLUSTRATION</small>

Funding	50% of Plans Have BSR in Excess of:	75% of Plans Have BSR in Excess of:
> 20 yrs.	121%	97%
15–19 yrs.	113	91
10–14 yrs.	99	74
< 10 yrs.	73	54

CHART 4–2

PERCENTAGE OF PLANS WITH VBSR AT INDICATED LEVEL OR HIGHER
(Vertical Scale)

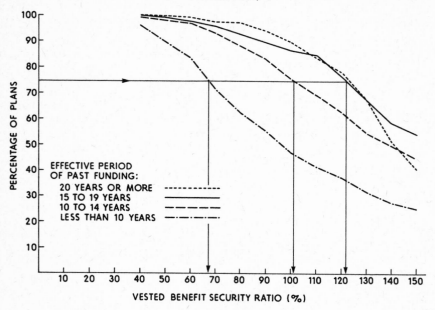

ILLUSTRATION

Funding	50% of Plans Have VBSR in Excess of:	75% of Plans Have VBSR in Excess of:
> 20 yrs.	140%	123%
15–19 yrs.	155	122
10–14 yrs.	138	101
< 10 yrs.	96	67

Average security ratios (BSR's and VBSR's) of the plans in the study are set forth in Table 4–2 according to the effective period of past funding. These are derived from adjusted ratios (maximum 100 percent for any plan) weighted by the value of total accrued benefits or vested accrued benefits, as the case may be.

Except for a deviation from trend caused by one large relatively poorly funded plan at a high funding duration, there is a steady progression upward, with duration, of the weighted average security ratios. As noted in connection with Table 1–2 of Chapter 1, the weighted average BSR's appear to have reached a high plateau after slightly more than 15 years of effective funding.

TABLE 4–2

AVERAGE SECURITY RATIOS BY EFFECTIVE PERIOD OF PAST FUNDING

Effective Period of Past Funding	Weighted Averages Based on Adjusted Ratios*	
	BSR	VBSR
Less than 10 years†	62.4%	68.3%
10–14 years	86.6	94.1
15–19 years	95.9	98.2
20–24 years	94.8	99.2
25–29 years	97.4	99.2
30 years or more	89.6‡	99.9
All periods combined	84.9%	90.2%

* Individual plan ratios limited to a maximum of 100 percent, and weighted in the averages by the value of accrued (or vested) benefits. These ratios are indicative of overall benefit security reached, but not of the ratios achieved by individual plans.

† All plans in this grouping have been in process of funding for at least 10 years.

‡ Excluding the one large case referred to in the preceding paragraph, this ratio is 99.5 percent. The presence of this particular case will not be further noted in the tables which follow.

The remaining tables in this chapter display security ratios by the following selected parameters combined with funding duration: size of plan (in terms of number of participants), scope of coverage, type of pension formula, type of funding instrument, vesting classification, and current funding practice. In these displays, composite security ratios for all durations combined have not been shown since these, by themselves, do not afford a proper basis of comparing plan groupings having substantially different distributions according to duration. Instead, tables of average BSR's and VBSR's are accompanied by tables showing a "security index" for the plan groupings under each parameter.

A plan's security index is obtained by dividing its unadjusted security ratio by the weighted average unadjusted security ratio of all plans at the same effective funding duration. For example, if a plan has an unadjusted security ratio of 117 percent and all plans at the same duration have an average unadjusted ratio of 130 percent, the plan in question has a security index of 90 percent (i.e., $117 \div 130 = .90$). The average security index for any particular grouping of plans is obtained by weighting the individual plan indices by their respective accrued benefit values. The security index thus equalizes for duration by indicating how the funding of a particular plan or grouping of plans compares with that of all plans of the same duration.

Size of Plan

Table 4–3A sets forth average security ratios according to size of plan, in three broad categories. A relatively smooth progression by duration is apparent for each size category. Also apparent is the fact that both the largest and smallest categories consistently surpass the medium sized category both in the BSR's and VBSR's (with one exception in each case).

TABLE 4–3A

SECURITY RATIOS ACCORDING TO SIZE OF PLAN

Effective Period of Past Funding	*Number of Participants per Plan*		
	Fewer than 1,000	*1,000–4,999*	*5,000 or more*
	Weighted Average BSR's		
Less than 10 years	65.7%	62.2%	62.3%
10–14 years	83.9	73.0	89.5
15–19 years	93.7	91.9	97.0
20–24 years	94.9	93.0	95.3
25–29 years	95.3	85.9	98.9
30 years or more	99.1	92.9	89.3
	Weighted Average VBSR's		
Less than 10 years	68.6%	73.1%	67.9%
10–14 years	92.8	87.9	95.1
15–19 years	97.2	96.4	98.7
20–24 years	99.0	98.3	99.5
25–29 years	99.0	92.1	100.0
30 years or more	100.0	98.8	100.0

A finer breakdown by size of plan reveals that the smallest plans (fewer than 100 participants) tend to have reached higher security ratios than others at durations under 10 years, and the largest plans (25,000 or more participants) tend to have reached higher security ratios at all longer durations. The former circumstance is probably due to the prevalence of conservative funding practices among such plans (frequently as to cost methods as well as assumptions). A further breakdown of Table 3–13 by size of plan (a breakdown not included among the tables displayed in this book) indicates that the latter circumstance may be due to higher past investment earnings associated with greater diversification of investment under large plans which typically employ funding media permitting equity investment.

Table 4–3B presents the relative index of benefit security according to size of plan.

TABLE 4–3B

INDEX OF BENEFIT SECURITY ACCORDING TO SIZE OF PLAN
("Equalized" for Duration)

Size of Plan (Number of Participants)	BSR Index	VBSR Index
Fewer than 1,000	1.02	1.11
1,000 but fewer than 5,000	0.95	1.04
5,000 or more	1.01	.99
All plans	1.00	1.00

Scope of Coverage

Security ratios for various coverage breakdowns are shown in Table 4–4A. Again the table has been divided into two parts, the first showing average security ratios according to scope and duration, and the second showing the relative index for various coverage breakdowns after "equalizing" for duration.

It is apparent from the last two sections of Table 4–4A that multiemployer plans of the Taft–Hartley type are of relatively recent origin, and that plans at the longer durations which were reported for the study as "multiemployer" were in fact plans covering associated employers. It is also apparent that

TABLE 4-4A

SECURITY RATIOS BY SCOPE OF COVERAGE

Effective Period of Past Funding	Weighted Average BSR's Plans Covering			Weighted Average VBSR's Plans Covering		
	Hourly Employees Only	Salaried Employees Only	All Employees	Hourly Employees Only	Salaried Employees Only	All Employees
Less than 10 years	62.1%	62.2%	64.7%	67.6%	84.7%	66.6%
10–14 years	72.5	89.5	92.9	81.8	96.7	99.4
15–19 years	83.3	96.1	96.7	91.7	97.3	99.2
20–24 years	88.6	95.3	95.2	94.0	99.4	99.8
25–29 years	82.3	92.4	98.4	99.9	94.6	99.9
30 years or more	100.0	99.4	88.8	100.0	100.0	99.9
	Bargained Plans	Plans Not Bargained		Bargained Plans	Plans Not Bargained	
Less than 10 years	60.9%	75.2%		66.5%	90.5%	
10–14 years	82.8	91.4		91.7	97.6	
15–19 years	93.4	96.7		98.7	98.1	
20–24 years	91.8	95.6		98.2	99.5	
25–29 years	97.4	97.4		99.2	99.2	
30 years or more	83.3	99.0		100.0	99.9	
	Single-Employer Plans	Multiemployer Plans		Single-Employer Plans	Multiemployer Plans	
Less than 10 years	64.3%	38.9%		69.2%	53.7%	
10–14 years	88.2	64.6		95.4	75.8	
15–19 years	95.9	98.9		98.2	99.8	
20–24 years	94.8	99.8		99.2	100.0	
25–29 years	97.4	100.0		99.2	100.0	
30 years or more	89.6	94.3		99.9	100.0	
	Multiemployer Bargained	All Other Plans		Multiemployer Bargained	All Other Plans	
Less than 10 years	38.3%	64.4%		53.0%	69.2%	
10–14 years	61.8	88.3		73.4	95.4	
15–19 years	100.0	95.9		100.0	98.2	
20–24 years	...	94.8		...	99.2	
25–29 years	...	97.4		...	99.2	
30 years or more	...	89.6		...	99.9	

there is a disparity between the security ratios of multiemployer plans and single-employer plans, primarily at the durations where Taft–Hartley plans predominate. Further information relating to this question may be found in Table 4–8.

TABLE 4–4B

INDEX OF BENEFIT SECURITY ACCORDING TO SCOPE OF COVERAGE
("Equalized" for Duration)

Scope of Coverage	BSR Index	VBSR Index
Plans covering hourly employees only	0.94	0.92
Plans covering salaried employees only ...	0.97	0.97
Plans covering all employees	1.05	1.06
All plans	1.00	1.00
Bargained plans	0.97	0.97
Plans not bargained	1.03	1.03
All plans	1.00	1.00
Single-employer plans	1.01	1.01
Multiemployer plans	0.76	0.77
All plans	1.00	1.00
Multiemployer bargained	0.71	0.72
All other plans	1.01	1.01
All plans	1.00	1.00

Type of Pension Formula

Table 4–5A indicates that plans providing a definite benefit formula exhibit higher security ratios, on the average, than plans which are based on a fixed contribution rate. This, in turn, is due primarily to the existence of substantially lower security ratios on the "cents-per-hour" plans, which are generally the multiemployer (or Taft–Hartley) plans. One other area of low security ratios may be noted—namely, plans providing a fixed dollar benefit not related to length of service. This latter classification is also weighted heavily by multiemployer plans.

TABLE 4–5A

SECURITY RATIOS BY TYPE OF PENSION FORMULA

| | | Defined Benefit Plans | |
Effective Period of Past Funding	Defined Contribution Plans	Service Related	Not Service Related
	Weighted Average BSR's		
Less than 10 years	52.4%	63.8%	34.0%
10–14 years	82.2	87.8	59.0
15–19 years	100.0	96.0	89.0
20–24 years	91.4	95.0	90.8
25–29 years	100.0	97.4	97.3
30 years or more	91.2	89.5	...
	Weighted Average VBSR's		
Less than 10 years	67.8%	69.4%	41.3%
10–14 years	99.8	95.0	70.6
15–19 years	100.0	98.3	95.7
20–24 years	95.4	99.4	97.1
25–29 years	100.0	99.2	97.3
30 years or more	98.5	100.0	...

TABLE 4–5B

INDEX OF BENEFIT SECURITY ACCORDING TO
TYPE OF PENSION FORMULA
("Equalized" for Duration)

Type of Pension Formula	BSR Index	VBSR Index
Defined contribution plans		
% of compensation	0.99	1.01
¢ per hour	0.68	0.82
All defined contribution plans	0.95	0.99
Defined benefit plans		
Service related		
% of final compensation	1.03	1.07
% of career compensation	1.04	1.00
Flat $ amount	0.94	0.93
All service related	1.01	1.01
Not service related		
% of compensation	1.05	1.31
Flat $ benefit	0.59	0.55
All not service related	0.75	0.76
All defined benefit plans	1.00	1.00
All plans	1.00	1.00

Type of Funding Instrument

Table 4–6A indicates that individually allocated funding instruments (typically plans insured through individual policies, group permanent contracts or deferred group annuities) have the highest security ratios. This is due in part to the presence of so-called level premium funding under many of these plans, and may also be due in part to more conservative funding assumptions. Another relationship which might be mentioned is the tendency of bargained plans to use unallocated funding instruments.

TABLE 4–6A.   Security Ratios by Type of Funding Instrument

| | Type of Funding Instrument | | |
	I Individually Allocated Instruments	II Unallocated Instruments	III Combinations
Effective Period of Past Funding			
	Weighted Average BSR's		
Less than 10 years	98.1%	62.0%	100.0%
10–14 years	99.7	83.9	99.3
15–19 years	100.0	95.3	98.1
20–24 years	99.0	92.9	99.2
25–29 years	100.0	96.7	99.9
30 years or more	99.8	86.2	100.0
	Weighted Average VBSR's		
Less than 10 years	99.0%	67.9%	100.0%
10–14 years	99.8	92.8	99.6
15–19 years	100.0	97.9	99.8
20–24 years	99.6	99.0	100.0
25–29 years	100.0	98.9	100.0
30 years or more	100.0	99.9	100.0

TABLE 4–6B.   Index of Benefit Security according to Type of Funding Instrument ("Equalized" for Duration)

Type of Funding Instrument	BSR Index	VBSR Index
I. Individually allocated instruments	1.08	1.02
II. Unallocated instruments	0.99	1.01
III. Allocated and unallocated combinations	1.00	0.93
All plans	1.00	1.00

Vesting Classification

Table 4–7A indicates little of significance in the relative security ratios (BSR's) according to vesting classification, but, as would be expected, reveals an inverse correlation between relative VBSR's and the liberality of vesting.

TABLE 4–7A. SECURITY RATIOS BY VESTING CLASSIFICATION

Effective Period of Past Funding	Vesting Classification		
	Early	Intermediate	Late
	Weighted Average BSR's		
Less than 10 years	65.6%	55.8%	65.2%
10–14 years	90.0	92.4	67.9
15–19 years	96.7	95.7	94.1
20–24 years	99.7	91.8	95.1
25–29 years	89.8	98.4	99.2
30 years or more	99.3	99.9	66.4
	Weighted Average VBSR's		
Less than 10 years	67.5%	64.9%	93.9%
10–14 years	91.9	96.9	91.0
15–19 years	98.3	97.3	99.6
20–24 years	100.0	98.6	100.0
25–29 years	94.1	100.0	100.0
30 years or more	99.9	100.0	100.0

TABLE 4–7B. INDEX OF BENEFIT SECURITY ACCORDING TO VESTING CLASSIFICATION
("Equalized" for Duration)

Vesting Classification	BSR Index	VBSR Index
Early	0.99	0.93
Intermediate	1.03	1.01
Late	0.96	1.24
All plans	1.00	1.00

Tables 4–8, 4–9 and 4–10 show relative security indices only, according to the following parameters:

Table 4–8: Scope of Coverage and Funding Instrument

Table 4–9: Current Funding Practice

Table 4–10: Investment Practice (as to Equity Investment)

Table 4–8 tends to support conclusions derived from Tables 4–4 and 4–6. However, in this table as well as in Table 4–6, the statistics are heavily concentrated in the unallocated funding instrument class. Accordingly, some of the breakdowns of the other funding instrument classes involve very few plans and therefore the results are subject to accidental fluctuation. This is particularly true of the breakdowns involving multi-employer plans—for example, only one plan (and that a small one) appears in the result shown in the allocated funding instrument column for "multiemployer bargained" plans.

Table 4–9 suggests that *current* funding practice (the item reported by participating firms and insurance companies) in many cases may be indicative of *past* practice. This conclusion appears to be supported by the correlation between the degree of conservatism in current practice and the relative security index.

Table 4–10 sets forth the relative security indices according to degree of investment in equities. It appears that this has not been a factor of overwhelming significance, although there are extraneous factors at work which tend to obscure the effect of investment policy alone. The group of plans having the least investment in equities (which group includes all insured plans of the allocated funding instrument type) exhibit a BSR index of 1.00. At the other end of the scale, plans having 56 percent or more of their assets invested in equities, show the highest BSR index—namely, 1.04. The authors have no ready explanation for the lower BSR index of 0.94 applicable to plans whose current percentage investment in equities falls in between, except to cite, in partial explanation, that there is a disproportionate weighting of multiemployer bargained plans in this particular classification.

TABLE 4–8

INDEX OF BENEFIT SECURITY ACCORDING TO COVERAGE AND FUNDING INSTRUMENT
("Equalized" for Duration)

Coverage	BSR Index			VBSR Index		
	Type of Funding Instrument			Type of Funding Instrument		
	Allocated	Unallocated	Combinations	Allocated	Unallocated	Combinations
Hourly employees only	1.08	0.94	0.87	1.10	0.92	1.21
Salaried employees only	1.06	0.97	0.91	0.98	1.02	0.86
All employees	1.11	1.04	1.07	1.07	1.07	0.99
Bargained	1.09	0.97	1.00	1.01	0.98	0.90
Not bargained	1.08	1.03	1.00	1.02	1.05	0.94
Single employer	1.08	1.01	1.00	1.02	1.02	0.93
Multiemployer	1.27*	0.75	0.88	1.22*	0.76	1.74
Multiemployer bargained	1.33*	0.71	...	4.14*	0.72	...
All other	1.08	1.01	1.00	1.02	1.02	0.93

* See comment on page 59.

TABLE 4–9

INDEX OF BENEFIT SECURITY ACCORDING TO
CURRENT FUNDING PRACTICE
("Equalized" for Duration)

Current Funding Practice	BSR Index	VBSR Index
Normal cost		
Being met in full	1.00	1.00
Not being met in full*	0.49	0.42
All plans	1.00	1.00
Supplemental cost		
Already fully funded†	1.05	1.02
Funded regularly in relatively		
uniform installments‡	1.00	0.99
Funded irregularly in nonuniform		
installments	1.07	1.12
Payment of interest only	0.80	0.83
Terminal funding	0.23	0.19
Other	1.04	0.99
All plans	1.00	1.00

* Only 7 cases out of 1,047 were so reported.

† According to cost method in use. A total of 88 cases out of 1,047 were so reported. A much larger number of plans (567) have accrued benefits fully funded (i.e., BSR of at least 100 percent).

‡ Including those reported as using cost methods that do not employ the supplemental cost concept, but which typically fund in relatively uniform installments.

TABLE 4–10

INDEX OF BENEFIT SECURITY ACCORDING TO
PERCENT INVESTED IN EQUITIES
("Equalized" for Duration)

Percentage of Assets Invested in Equities	BSR Index	VBSR Index
0–25	1.00	1.00
26–55	0.94	0.98
56–100	1.04	1.02
All plans	1.00	1.00

Chapter 5

Study Results in Terms of Funding Benchmarks

The importance of the effective period of past funding in the interpretation of the security ratios must be continually emphasized. If a particular case were to show a BSR of 90 percent and another 60 percent, very little meaningful interpretation could be drawn from these two percentages alone; it is only after the determination of effective period of past funding that relative funding progress can be examined. For example, if the effective period of past funding for both were 10 years, one might conclude that the 90 percent BSR situation had to date made the greater funding progress; but if the 60 percent case had been in the funding process for only five years, one might well reach the opposite conclusion.

In Chapter 4 the problem of recognizing differences in effective period of past funding in drawing comparisons between plans, or between groups of plans, has been attacked by

1. Grouping together in many of the tables plans with similar effective periods of past funding, and
2. By devising a benefit security index computed through use of a duration equalizer.

Even so, BSR's in Chapter 4 are expressed in relation to an absolute of 100 percent, a level which no plan can be expected to meet in its early years.

To avoid possible misinterpretation arising from the 100 percent absolute inherent in Chapter 4 results, the authors would like to give some indication as to how funding has progressed in relation to some guide line or series of benchmarks indicative of reasonable funding progress. If along a time line such benchmarks could be established, the ratios between the actual BSR's and those of the benchmark would become an index of funding progress in which 100 percent could be viewed as "on target."

The problem encountered here is a difficult one. There are no agreed upon standards of normal funding progress, and there appears to be no solid theoretical framework from which definite standards can be derived. Arbitrary benchmarks are likely to satisfy no one completely; yet they are unavoidable if the problem is to be faced. The authors have no particular insight into what constitutes reasonable progress, other than an awareness of the general shape of the BSR curve for various actuarial cost methods applied to employee groups with varying degrees of maturity.

The authors have devised two different sets of benchmarks for the limited purposes of this chapter; but they accept neither as a measure of what any particular funding pattern "ought to" look like, or that the funding of any particular plan ought to fit any pattern at all. The benchmarks chosen do fit the main characteristics of BSR graphs under typical actuarial cost methods, one fitting the relatively mature employee group, the other the relatively immature.

The first of the benchmarks has the mathematical form of a straight line rising from 0 to 100 percent over n years. The straight line is the simplest possible mathematical form; and, in addition, is a reasonably good fit to the funding pattern that develops if the original employee group is *mature* (including a full complement of retired lives). Chart 5–1 compares the straight line over n years with the BSR pattern that develops under the accrued benefit cost method if the original supplemental cost is funded by level annual payments over n years. A mathematical model devised and published by one of the authors[1] to represent the initially mature situation was used in drawing the BSR curve in Chart 5–1. The curve between 0 and n is bowed downward—i.e., it lies slightly below the straight line—because the portion of the level annual payment available for reducing the unfunded supplemental cost is smaller at first, but grows larger as the interest needed de-

CHART 5–1

BSR PROGRESS OVER TIME

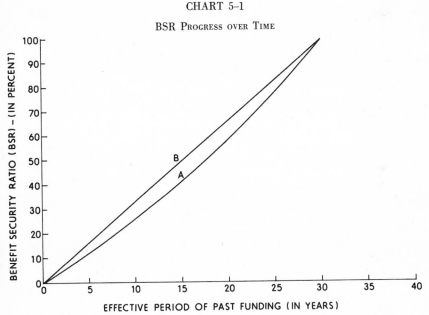

A. Initially mature model—accrued benefit cost method—30-year funding of supplemental cost.

B. Benchmark 1.

---

[1] Charles L. Trowbridge, "Fundamentals of Pension Funding," *TSA*, Vol. IV, 1952, pp. 17–43.

creases. The model assumes no change in benefits, but if benefit liberalizations were to be recognized the curve would be
generally above the level shown, and hence even closer to the
straight line.

The arbitrary factor in Benchmark 1 lies in the determination of n, the period over which the 100 percent level is attained. The authors have chosen 30 years, and accordingly
Chart 5–1 is drawn with $n = 30$. Many negotiated plans are bargained such that any supplemental liability is funded over 30
years, and 30 years is well within the range over which the supplemental cost is usually amortized.

The second benchmark is intended as a rough fit to the
initially *immature* situation. Curve C of Chart 5–2 shows the
BSR curve that develops if the initially mature model illustrated in Chart 5–1 is replaced by the initially immature model
from the same paper. Between 0 and n the accrued benefit cost
method BSR curve is now well above the straight line. The
bowedness-upward arises because the additional supplemental
cost developing as the group matures is 100 percent funded
through the the payment of current-service costs, and the effect
of adding a 100 percent funded part into the funding mix over-
powers the bowed-downward characteristics of the funding of
the original supplemental cost. The degree to which the BSR
curve is bowed-up depends on the degree of initial immaturity.

For Benchmark 2 the authors have chosen the simplest
second degree curve, that of the parabolic form $x^2 = y/n$,
where x is the security ratio benchmark, y is the effective period
of past funding, and n is the point at which the 100 percent BSR
is reached. As shown in D of Chart 5–2, this benchmark curve
is a little below the curve from the initially immature model.
One can view Benchmark 2 as representing a situation a little
more mature than in the mathematical model; or, he can view
it as representing the situation where benefit liberalizations

CHART 5–2

BSR Progress over Time

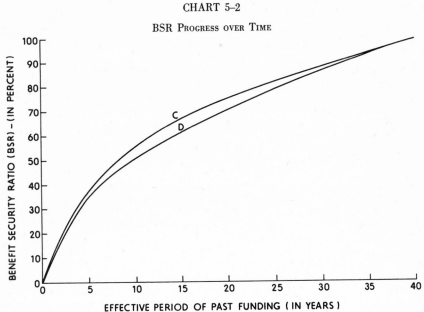

C. Initially immature model—accrued benefit cost method—40-year funding of supplemental cost.

D. Benchmark 2.

occur periodically, since (as in the initially mature situation) the effect of benefit increases is to make the funding pattern move closer to the benchmark.

The authors have chosen an n of 40 years for Benchmark 2, somewhat longer than the 30 years used with Benchmark 1. Chart 5–2 is therefore drawn with $n = 40$, and the amortization of the original supplemental liability is illustrated in Chart 5–2 on a 40-year basis.

Despite the somewhat longer n used with the immature model, the resulting Benchmark 2 is higher than Benchmark 1 during the first 22 years. Eighty-seven percent of the plans in

Part II of the study have effective periods of past funding of 22 years or less. After the crossing (where $y = 22.5$ years and both benchmarks are 75 percent) Benchmark 1 is the higher standard. Chart 5–3 illustrates on the same time line each of the two benchmarks.

CHART 5–3

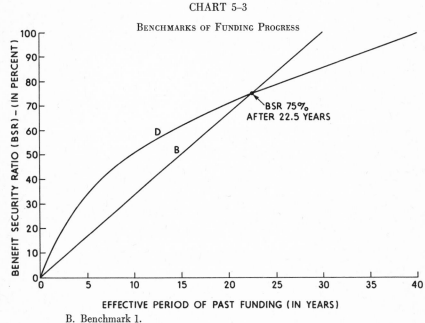

BENCHMARKS OF FUNDING PROGRESS

B. Benchmark 1.
D. Benchmark 2.

For each of the 1,047 plans in the study the actual BSR was related to the point on the benchmark graphs determined by the effective years of past funding for that particular plan. The results are summarized in Table 5–1. It will be noted that BSR's exceed Benchmark 1 in 94 percent of the 1,047 plans, and Benchmark 2 in nearly 90 percent.

TABLE 5–1

SECURITY RATIOS IN RELATION TO BENCHMARKS

BSR as a % of the Benchmark	Benchmark 1		Benchmark 2	
	Number of Plans	% of Plans at or above Level Indicated	Number of Plans	% of Plans at or above Level Indicated
Less than 50%	9	100.0%	11	100.0%
50–74	11	99.1	32	98.9
75–99	43	98.1	67	95.9
100–124	68	94.0	106	89.5
125–149	96	87.5	158	79.4
150–174	134	78.3	190	64.3
175–199	129	65.5	211	46.1
200 and up	557	53.2	272	26.0
All	1,047		1,047	
Average ratio BSR to benchmark				
Unweighted 226.0%			171.6%	
Weighted 177.3%			156.7%	

The unweighted average of the BSR to benchmark ratio shown on Table 5–1 is simply the mean of the distribution shown, and treats each plan equally. The weighted average recognizes that some of the plans in the study are much larger than others, and applies the appropriate weights. The weighted average can be viewed as the ratio of total assets from all plans to the assets that would exist if the funding of each plan were exactly on the benchmark.

The benchmarks devised for this paper were not expected to fit the data. They were established before the data were examined, and the rationale behind each is independent of what the results show. The reader may be interested in what benchmark would have resulted had the intent been to fit a benchmark to the data. Table 5–1 clearly indicates that the benchmark of best fit would be at a considerably higher level than either of the two chosen, but would depend upon whether best fit is measured by adjusted or unadjusted ratios and by weighted or unweighted averages. Those interested enough to plot the results of Table 1–2 on Chart 5–3 will discover that the benchmark of best fit would have bowed-upward characteristics, thus bearing out the original concept that the authors had in devising Benchmark 2—that the empirical graph of funding progress is likely to be bowed-upward because the initially immature situation is the one most often encountered in the practical situation.

Chapter 6

Interpretation

Accuracy To Be Attributed to
Benefit Security Ratios

In the design of this study the authors took all practicable precautions to avoid either overstatement or understatement of the benefit security ratios. Choices on details had to be made, however, and in several respects absolute technical accuracy was not possible. When choices were necessary, the authors leaned toward understatement of the security ratios rather than overstatement. In order that the reader can make his own interpretation of the results, a discussion follows as to the areas where approximations exist, and as to problems of interpretation in connection with the effect of certain parameters on the funding results.

Possible Overstatement of Accrued Benefits. Most benefit formulae common in pension plans lend themselves to the accurate calculation of benefits accrued to date. As an exception to this general statement, however, plans with benefits based on final-average salary normally define accrued benefits in terms of a moving-average not immediately available from normal salary records without special calculation. For such plans the instructions suggested use, for the accrued benefit calculation, of the more readily available pay on the determination date, with a resulting overstatement of accrued benefits. When accrued benefits are overstated, both types of benefit security ratio are understated. This understatement is probably not particularly significant in the overall, though with respect to certain plans (particularly where long averaging periods are combined with a recent history of rapid salary increase) the distortion may easily be on the order of 10 to 15 percent.

Approximation Due to Timing. As indicated in Chapter 2, the market value of assets (the numerator of the security ratios) was determined as of a current valuation date convenient for the actuarial firm, about 90 percent of the cases having such dates falling between October 1, 1965 and March 31, 1967. On the other hand, the present value of accrued benefits (the denominator of the security ratios) was based on an average of life company annuity rates determined as of March, 1966, which was approximately the mean of the valuation dates for all plans.

Chart 6–1 illustrates, along the same time line but on different vertical scales, (*a*) Standard & Poor's 500 Stock Price Index (monthly averages), (*b*) Standard & Poor's Bond Yield Index (monthly averages for long-term medium-grade (BBB) bonds), and (*c*) in bar chart form the distribution of plan valuation dates weighted by total accrued benefit values.

Clearly long-term interest rates showed a steady rise over the period of the study (with one downswing in early 1967) while the trend of stock market prices was relatively flat, despite variations in both directions.

Since the average valuation date (weighted by the security ratio denominators) was very close to the March, 1966 date as of which annuity rates were obtained (see Table 3–14), overall BSR and VBSR results should not be materially affected by timing differences. For any particular plan, however, the benefit security ratios may be *understated* if the valuation

CHART 6–1

STANDARD & POOR'S 500 STOCK PRICE INDEX;
STANDARD & POOR'S LONG-TERM BOND YIELDS (BBB)
TOGETHER WITH
DISTRIBUTION OF ACCRUED BENEFIT VALUES BY VALUATION DATE
1/1/65 TO 12/31/67
(See Table 3–14)

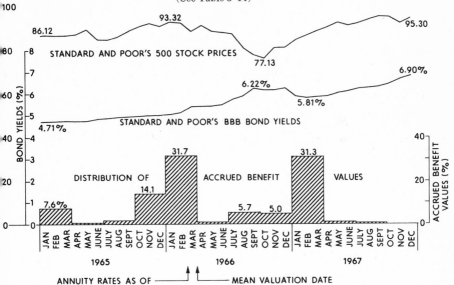

date falls after March, 1966, and overstated if the valuation date falls before that date, because the market value of fixed income securities is based on a current interest rate generally rising over the period of the study while the rate reflected by the insurance companies in the setting of the annuity rates was at the March, 1966 level.

The benefit security ratios will also vary with stock market prices. The effect here is not really a matter of understatement or overstatement, but rather a reflection of the changing level of benefit security inherent in market valuation of common stocks.

Combining these two effects, one might expect cases with late 1966 valuation dates to show relatively low security ratios because stock values were down and bond yields were high. Conversely, late 1965 cases might show relatively high security ratios due to a high stock market coupled with low bond yields. At certain other times the effect of stock prices and bond yields tend to cancel each other out. The effects suggested above, if actually present, are obscured by other BSR variation and do not appear to be demonstrable from the data.

It is the authors' opinion that the timing differences discussed here are not material to the interpretation of overall results. In any comparisons of security ratios between two classes of cases, however, the results could be distorted, if the average valuation date of either group varies significantly from March, 1966.

Possible Overstatement in Effective Years of Funding. As pointed out in Chapter 2, the effective years of funding calculated for each Part II case may be overstated because, in accordance with instructions, benefit liberalizations occurring more than 10 years prior to the valuation date, as well as any more recent liberalization of less than 10 percent, were ignored. There may well have been some underreporting of benefit increases as well, particularly those taking the form of liberalized vesting, which would have the same effect. Any overstatement of the effective years of funding would in no way affect the BSR or the VBSR with respect to the case in question; but it could affect the classification of the case in tables such as 4–2 through 4–7, and would certainly adversely affect the comparison of the case with either of the benchmarks. The tendency is to depress the ratios with respect to the benchmark, by increasing the number of years at which the benchmark curve is entered.

Underrepresentation of Certain Plans. As suggested in Chapters 1 and 2, the authors have reason to believe that certain classes of plan are underrepresented in the Part II data. Such underrepresentation in no way affects the BSR or the VBSR for any individual plan included within the study. There is no reason to assume that it affects in any material way the BSR's or VBSR's computed for the particular class underrepresented, unless the sample for the underrepresented class is thought to be too small. There is need to qualify the results, however, with respect to composite ratios which include in one result both the well-represented and underrepresented classes, if the underrepresented classes have atypical BSR's or VBSR's.

One class known to be underrepresented is the small plan. The factors which cause this underrepresentation are discussed in Chapter 2. Table 4–3B and the commentary in connection therewith indicate that small plans tend to be more heavily funded than the larger plans at the shorter funding durations, though the differences cannot be viewed as major. Their underrepresentation tends, therefore, to lower composite benefit security ratios at the shorter durations. Particularly the weighted ratio cannot be very much affected, however, since small plans have relatively little effect on this particular composite ratio.

The second class known to be underrepresented is the bargained, multiemployer plan. Here Table 4–4B indicates that the class in question exhibits somewhat lower than average security ratios, and hence the underrepresentation of these plans in the sample has the effect of overstating the composite benefit security ratios, particularly the weighted ratio.

Underrepresentation of other classes or subclasses, unintended but possibly present nonetheless, could have an effect on the composite ratios in either direction, depending upon the characteristics of the BSR's and VBSR's of the particular class or subclass of cases. The authors view these as probably relatively unimportant.

Problems of Interpretation. A word of caution may be in order as to possible misinterpretation of the security ratios or other displays of Chapter 4 which relate to subgroupings of the data.

If a particular plan has a BSR of 80 percent, for example, it is correct to assume that 80 percent of the benefits accrued to date are secured by plan assets. It is incorrect to assume, however, that accrued benefits are 80 percent secured for every participant within that plan in the event of plan termination. In that event plan assets are customarily allocated on a priority basis, with higher priorities given to the older, longer service employees. A high proportion of the total benefit values are concentrated on such employees. Thus, in the example cited, it is probable that participants in the higher priority classes would have 100 percent security, while those with low priority (and a relatively small proportion of the total benefit values) would have little or none. The 80 percent represents an average based on all benefits but usually would not apply uniformly to individual participants. Similarly a VBSR of 90 percent represents an average based on all vested benefits, with some vested individuals in a priority position having 100 percent security and others little or none.

Caution must also be exercised in interpreting the funding effects of any of the parameters illustrated in Tables 4–3 through 4–10. As has been stated earlier, in Chapters 2 and 4, these parameters cannot be assumed to be independent; on the contrary, certain parameters have been shown to be closely interrelated. These relationships can well obscure the true effect of any single parameter on the benefit security ratios, which effect would be clearly revealed only if the interactive effect of the others could be eliminated. Where misinterpretations of this type seem particularly likely, the authors have attempted to draw attention to the other factors affecting the result. For obvious reasons, the authors consider the overall results of the study more reliable than the results relating to any subgrouping of the data.

Some Basic Conclusions

While it is not possible to provide *exact* answers as to the degree of benefit security already accomplished under private pension plans in the United States, either in terms of specific parameters or overall, certain facts emerge rather clearly.

1. As of the central date of this study, a very high degree of benefit security had been accomplished by a vast majority of the plans included in the study. (In most cases these plans are those qualified under Internal Revenue Service regulations and subject to those regulations.)

For example, assets accumulated to the date of valuation were sufficient, on the average, to cover 94.4 percent of all accrued benefits under plans whose effective funding periods were 15 years or more. (This is on the basis of adjusted weighted averages which limit each plan's BSR to a maximum of 100 percent.) Consistent results apply to plans at the other funding durations. Assets were, of course, sufficient to cover an even greater proportion of *vested* accrued benefits.

In evaluating the benefit security results, it should again be borne in mind that no discount whatever has been made for employee turnover in obtaining any of the benefit values.

2. Nearly 90 percent of the plans studied had developed BSR's in excess of the more stringent of the benchmarks of

funding progress used by the authors for illustrative purposes, and 94 percent had done so with respect to the 30-year straight line benchmark. Even allowing for possible deficiencies of the sample studied, it is probable that close to 90 percent of all private pension plans would have BSR's exceeding one or the other of such benchmarks. If a similar comparison is made with VBSR's, a higher proportion of plans (approximately 98 percent) would exceed the benchmarks.

The significance of these proportions can readily be appreciated when it is considered that if *average* security ratios fell right on the benchmark at all durations, only about half of the plans (weighted for benefit values) would exceed the benchmark, as compared with the 90 percent or more found in the study.

3. There is overwhelming evidence that sound programs of financing have been the rule. The summary of prevailing practices as to the amortization of supplemental costs and the regular payment of normal costs (Table 3–6) indicates that most plans are having their pension costs systematically funded, and the 15 percent or so whose supplemental costs are being funded "irregularly" have achieved as high a degree of funding as the more systematically funded plans.

Beyond that, however, is the fact that the degree of accomplished security is a good deal higher, on the average, than would have been expected solely on the basis of practices relating to the amortization of supplemental costs, supporting the conclusion that conservative assumptions and cost methods have also been employed in the funding of most private pension plans.

4. Of all the classifications for which separate summaries have been made (other than duration of funding), the one providing the most significant variation in results is the classification according to single or multiemployer plan. Benefit

security in terms of the measurements used in this study is significantly greater under single-employer plans than under multiemployer plans, particularly those of the "Taft–Hartley" type.

The authors believe there are good reasons why this should be so. Under Taft–Hartley plans a primary consideration is usually to provide, at a fixed contribution rate, close to maximum benefits from the outset of the plan—that is, to provide an adequate level of benefits for those already near retirement as well as for those on behalf of whom many years of contribution remain to be made. Equity among generations of pensioners may be felt to require striking an actuarial balance between future contributions and benefit costs on a very long-range basis (frequently by payment of normal cost and interest on unfunded past-service costs rather than amortization of past-service costs), and by use of "realistic," rather than "conservative," actuarial assumptions.

The fact that multiemployer plans suffer by comparison with single-employer plans obscures the fact that *both* types of plan may compare favorably with a reasonable benchmark of funding progress. Thus, if single-employer plans at a given duration averaged 150 percent of the benchmark for that duration, and multiemployer plans were only 70 percent as favorable, a majority of the latter plans would still exceed the benchmark. It may be observed that the combined result for multiemployer bargained plans in this study shows their average BSR's to be 109 percent of Benchmark 2 (all other plans combined averaging 158 percent of that benchmark).

Finally, in connection with any comparison of single and multiemployer plans, it might be borne in mind that the primary orientation of this study has been toward security in the event of plan termination. It may be argued that the chance of plan termination is reduced under a multiemployer or industrywide plan because of the multiplicity of participating firms and the bargaining power of a strong union. Certainly these are factors to be considered.

5. With regard to the extent of vesting found under private pension plans in this study, the *value* of vested accrued benefits constitutes 81 percent of the value of all accrued benefits. A somewhat lower percentage would apply to the *amount* of benefits vested, or to the proportion of participants who enjoy vesting, since vested benefits are concentrated at the higher attained ages, resulting in a higher average value for vested than for nonvested benefits.

Using the vesting classifications of "Early," "Intermediate" and "Late" defined in the study, about 27 percent of the plans have early vesting, embracing 47 percent of the participants and 51 percent of the benefit values. (The corresponding figures for late vesting are 31 percent by plans, 19 percent by participants, and 12 percent by benefit values.) These results indicate that larger plans have more favorable vesting provisions than do small plans. To some extent this may indicate that older plans, which on the average are the larger plans, have tended to liberalize vesting as funding has been accomplished over the years; or, perhaps, that union bargaining, which is present to a greater degree under large plans, has tended to bring about that result.

Variation Due to Individual Plan Characteristics

The security ratios developed for individual plans show considerable variation. The introduction by the authors of "security indices" in Chapter 4 and "funding benchmarks" in Chapter 5 was designed to recognize and equalize the effect of one particular variable—namely, funding duration. However, there remain a number of other variable factors having a different effect on the security ratios of individual plans. Among these factors are:

a) The age distribution of participants, which affects the rate at which a given level of funding will develop a high security ratio.
b) The extent of the past-service benefits under the particular plan, which affects the period over which it is practicable to amortize all accrued benefit costs.
c) The extent of recent benefit liberalizations, which have a dampening effect on the progress of security ratios.
d) The existence or nonexistence of bargaining under the particular plan, which has effects noted earlier.
e) Circumstances peculiar to the company or industry, a few of which are commented upon briefly below.

Benefit objectives and financing objectives vary between companies and plans. With regard to the former, in one case the "money purchase" or savings principle may be followed under which benefits for individual participants relate solely to contributions made for future service; under another, benefits may also be given for past service, the cost of which must be amortized over a future period. With regard to financing objectives, companies with relatively stable earnings may desire to amortize past-service costs by uniform payments over a fixed period, whereas companies with widely fluctuating earnings may wish to avail themselves of the flexibility permitted by Internal Revenue Service regulations, varying annual contributions in accordance with company earnings.

For reasons such as those mentioned above, there is a rather wide dispersion of security ratios in this study. Taking all plans included in Part II of the study, without breakdown according to any parameter, the BSR's vary from less than 40 percent to well over 160 percent. Almost 30 percent of the plans have BSR's below 80 percent, almost 40 percent of the plans have BSR's between 80 and 120 percent, and about one third of the plans have BSR's in excess of 120 percent.

This dispersion is not due solely to the effect of funding duration. As is apparent from Chart 1–2 of Chapter 1, there is a considerable dispersion of plans about the mean in every duration group. As the duration increases, there is of course a shifting of the entire distribution as the mean moves upward.

The true significance of an individual plan's security ratio will depend upon that plan's own investment earning power (as well as future experience as to other factors) rather than on the particular assumptions used to measure costs in this study. Even though a plan shows a BSR of 80 percent in this study, it may be that circumstances peculiar to that plan would translate the figure to 60 percent or 100 percent, or some other number, if its own future experience could be accurately projected.

Comparison with Earlier Study

The earlier pilot study of plans whose actuarial work was performed by a single firm (reported in *PCAPP*, Vol. XIV, pp. 128–38), which was a forerunner of the present study, produced comparable but somewhat higher security ratios. The results of the earlier study were all presented in terms of unadjusted, unweighted ratios—that is, each plan being given equal weight regardless of size and values in excess of 100 percent being reflected in the averages. Therefore, comparisons between the two studies must be made on the basis of such averages. Overall, this particular comparison is as follows:

	Earlier Pilot Study	Present Study
Average number of years plans had been in effect	16.6	17.0
Average BSR, all durations combined*	117.2%	101.7%
Percentage of plans with BSR > 100 percent, all durations combined	64.4%	54.2%

* Unadjusted, unweighted averages.

The following are the principal reasons for the differences found in the two studies:

a) Largely as a result of union negotiations, tremendous benefit increases occurred in the interval between studies, a circumstance
which automatically caused a "setback" in the accomplished security ratios. Although a device was adopted in the present study to
adjust the "effective funding period" for such increases, the absolute values of the security ratios were nonetheless reduced, not only
overall but for most groupings of plan by duration.

b) At the valuation dates of the present study, market values of assets
in relation to cost or book values were somewhat less favorable
than in the earlier study, particularly with respect to bonds.

c) Changes in the methodology adopted for the present study also
led to some reduction in security ratios. For example, in the present
study accrued benefits under plans relating benefits to "final average pay" were based on compensation at the valuation date, rather
than on a recent average of compensation prior to the valuation
date as in the earlier study. Also, the basis of valuing the cost of
accrued benefits in the present study corresponded to the average
of several leading company "close-out" rates, which produced a
little higher cost than the "best available rate" used at the time of
the earlier study.

d) Finally, there was obviously a different sample of plans involved
in the two studies, the earlier one having been smaller and limited
to plans serviced by a single actuarial consulting firm.

While the proportion of plans at all durations combined
which had already reached a BSR of 100 percent was higher
in the earlier study (64 versus 54 percent), the conclusions
reached concerning the proportion of plans whose funding was
ahead of a "reasonable benchmark" were similar in the two
studies.

General Observations

There can be little doubt that the high degree of benefit
security accomplished under private pension plans by the year

1966, as measured by the results of this study, is due in large measure to this country's having passed through two decades of rising interest rates. This has meant that contributions to pension plans during this period were made on a more conservative basis, on the whole, than the standards of measurement of benefit security considered to be appropriate in 1966. Other factors have also contributed to the same result—namely, the widespread use of actuarial cost methods which fund current-service costs more rapidly than they accrue, and favorable experience during this period with regard to capital appreciation on equity investments.

A similar test of benefit security performed 15 or 20 years from now might show somewhat different results. Aside from any changes in funding practice which may occur, if cost factors should increase in the future—as would result from a downturn in investment yields, higher expenses, or significantly decreased mortality—the funding margins created in the recent past, principally by a rather sharp upward swing in investment yields, would tend to disappear. Therefore, it should not be assumed that the highly satisfactory buildup of security ratios in the past will necessarily be characteristic of the future. Any performance objectives visualized for the future should take into account the important effect of what may be cyclical trends on the "benefit security ratio" measurement.

This study constitutes a "snapshot" of the status of private pension plan funding centered about the year 1966. As a single snapshot of the ever changing relationship between benefits and rate of funding which together make up benefit security, it is meaningful primarily in relation to snapshots taken at other points of time. The picture must of course be expected to change as new developments occur, whether these are in the form of expanded benefits and new funding procedures or in the form of changes in the economic, political, and social climate.

In the opinion of the authors, the principal message to be found in the results of this study is the clear evidence that during the past several decades, while the climate has been favorable to the independent development of private plans, these plans have responded with a remarkably healthy growth, both in the evolution of benefits and benefit forms and in the enhancement of employee security through sound financing.

This study also demonstrates a tremendous diversity in the private pension field. Unions and employers, operating on the basis of free bargaining and independent judgment, have arrived at decisions leading to the adoption of a wide variety of plan provisions and funding policies adapted to their special requirements. Since the possibility of satisfying diverse objectives is one of the principal reasons why private pension plans exist, the wide variation in results presumably should be viewed as normal and desirable.

Suggestions for Further Research

This pioneer study has produced quantitative results which, though lacking great refinement, are fairly accurate indicators of the levels of benefit security reached under private pension plans. As such an indicator, the study has responded to a need for information in a hitherto relatively unprobed area.

The authors suggest that a similar, perhaps more comprehensive study, be undertaken in a matter of 5 to 10 years, in an effort to establish a closer correspondence between funding results and a number of factors which vary according to the characteristics of individual plans. Such a study would also provide a second snapshot in what may eventually prove to be a series of snapshots designed to determine important funding trends. An attempt might also be made to determine the extent of benefit coverage under pay-as-you-go plans, whether providing the sole coverage or supplementing funded plans.

The authors also suggest the need for investigation and serious research on the funding of plans covering public employees. By comparison with private plans, it would appear that public plans are on the whole rather poorly funded; in fact, there are some public plans which, after making provision for employees already retired, fail to have sufficient assets to cover even the participants' own contributions. While somewhat different considerations apply to public than to private plans, there are nonetheless certain funding procedures which must be regarded as appropriate for all employers, public or private.

Appendix

Instructions to Participating Actuarial Firms and Insurance Companies

BASIC INFORMATION RELATIVE TO STUDY

Purpose of Study

The basic purpose of this study is to assemble information which will serve as a basis for an enlightened judgment as to whether employers and labor unions, as a group and in various categories, are pursuing financial policies that offer reasonable assurance that the benefit expectations of pension plan participants will be realized. The central item of information being sought is the actuarial value of the accrued benefits of a representative sample of private pension plans in operation for 10 years or more, classified according to various characteristics. These values will be compared to the respective asset accumulations to derive a so-called benefit security ratio for each plan in the sample and for various categories of plans. This approach is based upon the premise that the relationship as of any given date between the assets of a pension plan and the actuarial value of its accrued benefit obligations serves as the most meaningful and easily understood measure of the security attaching to such benefit accruals as of that time. Furthermore, this approach makes possible valid comparisons on a reasonably uniform basis of the funding progress under plans having heterogeneous characteristics and employing diverse actuarial cost methods as a guide to funding policy.

The use of this particular approach in this study does not question nor deny the validity of other measures of financial soundness developed under different assumptions and for other purposes.

General Procedures

The information essential to this study is to be furnished by the leading pension consulting firms and the life insurance companies which underwrite the bulk of insured pension plans. These cooperating firms will submit the information requested herein to the Pension Research Council of the Wharton School of Finance and Commerce, which will record the data on punched cards and perform the necessary statistical analysis. The analyses will be carried out under the supervision of the principal investigators, Messrs. Frank L. Griffin, Jr. of The Wyatt Company and C. L. Trowbridge of the Bankers Life Company. The results of the study will be published in book form by the Council under the coauthorship of Messrs. Griffin and Trowbridge.

Every precaution will be taken to preserve the confidentiality of data submitted in respect of any particular plan. Employers (and unions) will not be identified by name in any material submitted to the Council. Neither will any statistics be used in any reports or publications in such a manner as to permit identification of especially large plans. If the cooperating organizations have any fears or reservations on this point, however, they may divide all asset and liability figures submitted by a convenient divisor (not larger than five), provided only that the number of employees when divided by the same factor still falls within the same size *classification* as that of the undivided plan.

It is recognized that the valuation of certain types of benefits presents difficulties and that a variety of approaches may be used. In these areas, the Council is prepared to accept the judgment of the actuary who makes the regular valuations of the plan, in order to simplify the calculations and to minimize problems of liaison. In all cases, however, the procedures employed by the cooperating firms should be consistent with the spirit of this memorandum.

Scope of Study

The study is limited to plans currently covering 25 or more employees which have been in process of funding for a minimum of 10 years. These constraints were adopted for the purposes of (1) keeping the number of cases within manageable bounds, and (2) confining the examination to those plans that have had sufficient time to fund a substantial portion of the initial accrued liability. Even with these constraints, the number of cases appears to be too large to handle. Thus, it has been concluded that plans covering fewer than 1,000 employees should be subjected to a sampling technique, before seeking the detailed information relative to funding which is set forth in Part II of the questionnaire.

Information with respect to Part I of the questionnaire is to be completed for all plans falling within the scope of the study—namely, plans which have been in process of funding for a minimum of 10 years and which cover 25 or more employees—regardless of whether these plans are to be included in Part II. The information derived from Part I will be used to determine the "universe" of plans from which a valid sample will be derived for Part II. The plans to be reported in

Part II of the questionnaire will be selected by a process to be described in a subsequent memorandum.

Reporting Responsibility

In cases where there is overlapping jurisdiction, usually associated with split-funding arrangements, the reporting should be done by the firm which customarily brings together the various pieces of the actuarial valuation for the plan as a whole. In any case where this responsibility is not clearly delineated, it would be well for the consultant and insurance company to agree between themselves as to the overriding responsibility for reporting.

In almost all cases the information required by Part I of the questionnaire should be readily avaliable to the reporting firm or company. Should there be doubt about any item appearing on the reporting sheet, however, the information should be obtained from the appropriate source.

INFORMATION TO BE REPORTED IN PART I OF QUESTIONNAIRE

All information for Part I should be submitted on Reporting Sheet—Part I (p. 91), a supply of which can be obtained from the Pension Research Council. Where appropriate, data should be reported in accordance with the codes shown below. The following information should be reported:

A. *Contributing Firm or Insurance Company*

B. *Case or Plan Number.* In order to conceal the identity of the plans encompassed by the study, the consulting firm or insurance company should assign a number to each of the plans for which data are submitted and report the plans only by serial number.

INQUIRY INTO THE EXTENT OF FUNDING UNDER PRIVATE PENSION PLANS

Reporting Sheet—Part I

A. Contributing Firm or Insurance Company_____

B. Case or Plan Number   _____

Code

C. Occupational Classification of Employer   _____

D. Number of Participants in Plan   _____

E. Basic Type of Benefit Formula   _____

F. Funding Instrument   _____

G. Scope of Coverage   _____

H. Categories of Employees Covered   _____

I. Actuarial Cost Method Currently Used
   in Valuations   _____

J. Funding of Normal Cost   _____

K. Treatment of Supplemental Liability,
   if any   _____

L. Total Number of Years, past and future,
   over which funding of supplemental
   liability, if any, is expected to be
   accomplished   _____

M. Years Plan Has Been in Processing of
   Funding   _____

SEE MEMORANDUM OF INSTRUCTIONS

Initials_____

Date_____

C. *Occupational Classification of Employer or Union*

```
Manufacturing ........................... Code 1
Mining and Petroleum ..................... Code 2
Construction ............................. Code 3
Transportation ........................... Code 4
Communication and Utilities .............. Code 5
Wholesale and Retail Trade ............... Code 6
Finance, Insurance, and Real Estate ...... Code 7
Services ................................. Code 8
Unclassified ............................. Code 9
```

D. *Number of Participants.* "Participants" should be construed to include active employees, former employees with vested benefits, retired employees, and other persons currently receiving benefits under the plan. Do not include dependents or beneficiaries of employees in the count unless such persons are currently receiving benefits. The number of participants should be reported in size classifications in accordance with the following codes:

```
25 but fewer than 100 employees .......... Code 1
100 but fewer than 500 employees .......... Code 2
500 but fewer than 1,000 employees ........ Code 3
1,000 but fewer than 5,000 employees ........ Code 4
5,000 but fewer than 25,000 employees ....... Code 5
25,000 employees and over .................. Code 6
```

E. *Basic Type of Benefit Formula.* Identify the basic type of benefit formula in accordance with the following broad classifications. Combinations of two or more classifications should be reported by a two-digit code, the first digit of which in every case would be *3* and the second digit of which would correspond to the second digit of the dominant formula in the "20" series. (This procedure for coding combinations assumes that most combinations will involve formulas in the "20" series. The objective is to designate the dominant or controlling formula by the second digit of the combination code which utilizes the "30" series.)

```
Defined contribution plans
  Cents per hour .......................................... Code 11
  Percentage of compensation .............................. Code 12
Defined benefit plans
  Unit benefit, flat dollar amount ........................ Code 21
  Unit benefit, percentage of compensation, career average ..... Code 22
  Unit benefit, percentage of compensation, final average ....... Code 23
  Level percentage of compensation ........................ Code 24
```

Flat benefit, subject to minimum period of service .... Code 25
Combination formulas—see above statement

F. *Funding Instrument*

Individual insurance contract .... Code 1
Group permanent contract .... Code 2
Group deferred annuity .... Code 3
Group deposit administration annuity or IPG .... Code 4
Trust fund plan .... Code 5

(For a combination plan, code with two digits, showing the two instruments which currently predominate. For example, a combination of a group deposit administration annuity and trust fund would be coded as 45. Do not use three digits in any situation.)

G. *Scope of Coverage*

Single employer (may include more than one
employer if employers are all financially related)
Collectively bargained .... Code 11
Not collectively bargained .... Code 12
Multiemployer
Collectively bargained .... Code 21
Not collectively bargained .... Code 22

H. *Categories of Employees Covered*

Hourly only .... Code 1
Salaried only .... Code 2
All employees .... Code 3

I. *Actuarial Cost Method or Methods Currently Used in Regular Valuations*

Accrued benefit cost method
With supplemental liability .... Code 110
Without supplemental liability .... Code 120
Projected benefit cost method
Individual level cost
With supplemental liability .... Code 211
Without supplemental liability .... Code 212
Aggregate level cost
With supplemental liability .... Code 221
Without supplemental liability .... Code 222

The foregoing code system may be converted into earlier terminology for actuarial cost methods as follows:

Code 110—Single premium; unit cost; unit credit; or step-rate.
Code 120—No comparable method.
Code 211—Entry age normal.
Code 212—Attained age level premium; or attained age level
    contribution.
Code 221—Entry age normal; attained age normal; or frozen
    initial liability.
Code 222—Aggregate or percentage-of-payroll.

J, K, and L. *Funding Policy.* Items J, K, and L, collectively, are
designed to describe the funding policy for the plan. Item J seeks
to determine whether the *normal* costs of the plan are being funded
in full. If the answer is "Yes," as it presumably will be in most
cases, the numeral "1" should be entered under "Code." A negative
response should be indicated by the numeral "2."

Item K elicits information concerning the treatment of the
supplemental liability, if any, under the plan. This item is to be
answered only if the entry opposite item I shows Code 110, 211,
or 221. Responses to this query are to be reported in accordance
with the following codes:

Policy	Code
Funded at regular intervals in reasonably uniform installments	1
Funded at irregular intervals in nonuniform installments	2
Terminal funding	3
Payment of interest only	4
No funding nor payment of interest	5
Other (please describe briefly)	6

Code 1 is intended to reflect those situations where the employer
or union is following a predetermined pattern of funding designed
to produce a fully funded status within a given number of years.
The code is appropriate, however, where the employer is, *in fact*,
funding the supplemental liability in a systematic manner, whether
or not he is following a formal, articulated policy. Code 2 should be
used when the employer is not following a definite schedule of funding payments or when, in fact, contributions are determined by the
current fiscal position of the employer. Code 3 should be indicated
when the employer is following a policy of funding in a particular
year only the supplemental liability associated with the participants
who retire or reach the normal retirement age in that year. In
essence, this practice constitutes terminal funding of the supple-

mental liability. Code 4 is primarily designed to reflect a deliberate policy of meeting only the interest on the supplemental liability, but it should also be used when funding payments in the aggregate have only offset the interest accruals. If no payments of any sort have been made toward the supplemental liability, Code 5 should be shown.

Item L is designed to indicate the number of years that will elapse *since adoption of the present funding policy* before the supplemental liability will be fully funded, assuming no increase in the supplemental liability and assuming continuation of present funding policies.

M. *Years Plan Has Been in Process of Funding.* The study is limited to plans which have been in process of funding for 10 or more years. There may be some cases where it is difficult to assign a number to this item, because of the merger of one or more plans which have been in process of funding for differing periods. Where this is the case, an approximation based on the weighted average period for the respective merged plans (weighted by numbers of participants) will be satisfactory.

INFORMATION TO BE REPORTED IN PART II OF QUESTIONNAIRE

All information for Part II should be submitted on Reporting Sheet—Part II (p. 96), a supply of which can be obtained from the Pension Research Council. The first two items on this sheet are the same as those appearing on the sheet for Part I, for cross reference purposes. Other than these two items, the lettering follows in sequence from that in Part I.

Items of Information

N. *Point at Which Vesting Commences.* Enter on the Reporting Sheet the point at which vesting commences in accordance with the terms of the plan. This should be reported both in terms of years of service and attained age if both of these requirements are contained within the plan document.

INQUIRY INTO THE EXTENT OF FUNDING
UNDER PRIVATE PENSION PLANS

Reporting Sheet—Part II

A. Contributing Firm or Insurance Company_____

B. Case or Plan Number   _____

N. Point at Which Vesting Commences: Service____yrs.;
    Age____yrs.

O. Point at Which Vesting is Complete: Service____yrs.;
    Age____yrs.

P. Significant Benefit Increases in Last 10 Years:

	Date	*Approximate Percentage*
	_____	_____%
	_____	_____%
	_____	_____%
	_____	_____%

Q. Date of Valuation Used Herein   _____

R. Market Value of Assets on Valuation Date $_____
    % in Equities_____

S. Book Value of Assets on Valuation Date $_____
    % in Equities_____

T. Actuarial Value of Accrued Benefits:
    (*i*) Retired Participants $_____
    (*ii*) Terminated and Vested (not yet retired)   _____
    (*iii*) Active Participants, Vested   _____
    (*iv*) Active Participants, Nonvested   _____
    (*v*) Total—All Accrued Benefits $_____

U. Gross Actuarial Liability by Cost Methods and
    Assumptions in Current Use $_____

SEE MEMORANDUM OF INSTRUCTIONS

Initials_____
Date_____

O. *Point at Which Vesting Is Complete.* This item of information is relevant only to plans in which graded vesting is used. If graded vesting is not used, this entry will be the same as the one in N.

P. *Significant Benefit Increases in Last 10 Years.* The dates and approximate percentage increase are to be entered. A benefit increase should be considered "significant" if either the benefits themselves or the cost of the benefits were increased by 10 percent or more. If the true cost increase was not reflected in the contribution rate, due to a concurrent change in the actuarial assumptions, the percentage shown should be based on the change in average amount of benefits or on the change in contribution rate based on the assumptions previously in effect.

Q. *Date of Valuation Used.* It is contemplated that data will be reported as of the date of the regular valuation in 1966 (or 1965 if more convenient).

R. and S. *Reporting of Asset Values at Market and Book.* Assets are to be reported on both a market and a book value basis, except that in the case of individual insurance or annuity contracts, or group permanent contracts which are not experience rated, the cash value plus reserves for retired lives and paid-up benefits will constitute the asset value to be reported for both the market and book basis. For insured plans, other than those above, the measure of assets should be the experience fund on both a market and book basis, rather than the annual statement reserves. The market value of assets may be approximated from book values at the discretion of the reporting organization. The percentage of the assets on each basis, which are invested in equities, is to be shown opposite the dollar value of the assets. The asset values to be reported under the various funding instruments are as follows:

Trust Fund Plan: Asset values contained in the trustee's statement.
Group Annuity Contract, including *Deposit Administration:* Asset values reflected in the experience fund, including those applicable to retired lives.
Individual Insurance or Annuity Contracts: Cash values plus reserves for retired lives and paid-up benefits.

Group Permanent Contract: Asset values in experience fund, including those applicable to retired lives. If the contract is not experience rated, report cash values plus reserves for retired lives and paid-up benefits.

Any employer contributions made after the valuation date but applicable to the period ending with the valuation date are to be added to the assets. Employer contributions made prior to the valuation date, applicable to the period following the valuation date, are to be deducted from the assets. Benefit payments and investment income should likewise be adjusted to an accrual basis, if feasible.

T. *Actuarial Value of All Accrued Benefits.* All benefits are to be valued on a plan close-out basis as of the most recent date of valuation. Retirement or annuity benefits are to be valued on the basis of the factors shown at the end of this memorandum. These factors are based on representative rates currently being quoted by certain leading life insurance companies for the purchase of single premium deferred and immediate annuities in connection with the "close-out" of pension plans, with additional margins added in the interest of conservatism. Thus, they reflect an essentially "market" valuation of accrued benefits. Death benefits and other special benefits are to be valued on the basis of the commutation columns furnished. These values have been constructed on a basis consistent with the "close-out" annuity rates employed.

It is not expected that the "matured" benefits of subclassifications (*i*) or (*ii*) of this item T will cause any difficulty in most instances. On the other hand, the separation of accrued benefits and their values for active participants, between vested and nonvested in subclassifications (*iii*) and (*iv*), may not be readily available on an exact basis. In that event, these values may be separated on an approximate basis. For example, the cooperating firms or insurance companies may assume that, on the average, vesting under the particular plan takes place at age "X," thus eliminating the service requirement as such, or take such other short cut as may appear to be appropriate.

While the *amounts* of accrued benefits are to be computed as if the plan is being terminated, the extent to which such benefits have *vested* is to be determined in accordance with the plan provisions on the assumption that the plan is to continue in operation.

Determination of Accrued Benefits

It is recognized that the determination of accrued benefits as of any given time poses certain problems and involves many matters of judgment. If the plan provides for a specific unit of retirement benefits for each year of credited service, no problem of computation exists with respect to accrued *normal* retirement benefits. Even when the plan does not clearly define the accrued benefits as of any point in time, the early retirement or vesting provisions (if they are independent of funding patterns) may point to what the plan designer considers accrued benefits to be. Where the plan itself does not resolve the matter, or where there are special benefits to be valued, the guidelines in this memorandum should be followed. In all cases, reasonable approximations are acceptable. The *amount* of accrued benefits to be valued will be computed in accordance with the following guidelines:

1. Employees who, on the valuation date, have not met minimum service or age requirements for *eligibility* under the plan, are presumed not to be included in the valuation. If the waiting period is not credited in the determination of the benefit following eligibility, benefits should be assumed to start to accrue on completion of the waiting period. If the waiting period is credited in the benefit formula following eligibility, the accrued benefits of any employee who has satisfied the eligibility requirements should be assumed to include service during the waiting period.

2. If the employee could satisfy the minimum service requirement by his normal retirement date, his accrued benefits, computed in accordance with the procedures described earlier, should be reflected in the valuation. If he could not satisfy the minimum service requirement by his normal retirement date, he should not be included in the valuation.

3. Retired employees and terminated employees with vested benefits should be included in the valuation.

4. In general, accrued benefits are to be based upon the normal retirement benefit formula and, if applicable, the employee's service and earnings to the date of valuation.

Where there is not a definite benefit accrual for each year of service, the projected benefit at the assumed normal retirement date should be determined on a basis consistent with the instructions which follow, and the "accrued benefit" should be obtained by prorating the total projected benefit on the basis of years of service, as follows. The numerator of the fraction should be years of service (i) beginning upon completion of the initial eligibility period (or at date of hire if there is no initial waiting period or if such waiting period is later counted in computing the projected benefit at retirement), and (ii) ending upon the valuation date. The denominator of the fraction equals the numerator plus the years remaining from the valuation date to the assumed normal retirement date.

The above procedure establishes the amount of accrued benefits without regard to the vesting provisions of the plan. The amount of *vested* accrued benefits may be determined either by applying individual vesting percentages to each individual's total accrued benefits, or by an approximation such as, for example, the total accrued benefits with respect to all employees who are over an appropriately selected age. The use of a suitable approximation is left to the actuary's judgment.

5. "Final average earnings," where required, should be interpreted to mean earnings on the valuation date, except that any participant who is within the last half of the final period over which earnings are averaged may have his earnings on the valuation date appropriately adjusted, at the actuary's option.

6. Except where the benefit formula clearly defines an accrued or prior service benefit at any point of time, under formulas providing variable percentages of benefit for different periods of service (e.g., 2 percent of final average pay times years of service at retirement not in excess of 15 plus 1 percent times years of service in excess of 15), the benefit should be projected to normal retirement date and then prorated as indicated under (4) in order to obtain the accrued benefit. The same procedure is indicated where service credit is subject to a maxi-

mum or where there is no fixed relationship between the amount of benefit and the length of service.

7. Where there are various retirement ages with different benefits applicable (e.g., UAW vested pensions are deferred to age 65, but retirement on full benefits is possible at age 62 and there may be supplementation), it is suggested that the valuation assume that retirements all take place at an average age falling between (*i*) the normal retirement age and (*ii*) the age at which the pension has the greatest actuarial value to the employee, provided he would have been entitled to such benefit without employer consent at such age had he continued in employment. The selection of such an average age is left to the judgment of the actuary. Because of special situations and special circumstances, it is recognized that a different method of handling this problem may be used by the firm or company preparing and submitting the information, provided such method is consistent with the basic approach outlined.

8. Where early retirement benefits are greater than "actuarial equivalents," the added accrued early retirement benefit should be valued, with the method of doing so to be left to the judgment of the actuary.

9. Lump-sum benefits and large temporary annuities supplementing life pensions (e.g., Steelworkers 13-week benefit and UAW Supplemental Allowance), may be considered under (7) and (8) above if such benefits are funded as an integral part of the pension and would, if the plan continued, be paid to substantially all early or normal retirements. Otherwise, such benefits should not be considered.

10. Death benefits, including refunds of employee contributions, should be considered during the period of deferment of the pension. Post-retirement death benefits, including subsidized joint and survivor options, should likewise be considered if provided automatically from the pension fund for normal retirements.

11. Increased benefits for retirement under *special* conditions (e.g., UAW Special Early and Steelworkers layoff after rule of 75 or 80), should not be considered in the valuation unless in the judgment of the actuary they are sufficiently predictable to permit a cost estimate and of such a frequency as to affect costs materially.

12. The earned portion of any severance benefits in the pension plan which exceed the actuarial value of the accrued pension should

be considered in the valuation, with the method of doing so left to the judgment of the actuary.

13. Under individual policy and group permanent plans, accrued benefits and costs should be determined in the same manner as outlined above for other plans. In other words, in calculating accrued benefits under these plans, ignore the fact that benefits on termination or early retirement may be related to the funding pattern.

U. *Gross Actuarial Liability By Cost Method(s) and Assumptions in Current Use.* For any plan which uses a cost method involving a "supplemental liability" in addition to normal cost, report here the gross actuarial liability produced by the actuarial cost method(s) and assumptions currently used for valuing the liabilities of the plan. For plans using other cost methods, enter the phrase "equal to assets."

ACTUARIAL FACTORS FOR VALUATION OF ACCRUED BENEFITS

Attached hereto are certain commutation functions and annuity rates to be used in determining the values of accrued pension benefits and death benefits, if any, of the pension plans included within Part II of the Pension Research Council Inquiry into the Extent of Funding under Private Pension Plans.

These functions are based on the Ga 1951 Table (Male), without projection, 3¾% interest, and no loading. With the exception of the deferred and immediate annuity rates, which are set out for males and females separately, values for females are obtained by setting back the female age 5 years.

The deferred and immediate annuity rates obtained on the basis of these tables are the approximate equivalent of the median values of the gross "close-out" rates furnished by 12 insurance companies in reply to a recent questionnaire, and are therefore considered suitable for the purpose at hand.

Immediate Annuity Rates

Age	$\dfrac{N_x^{(12)}}{D_x}$ Males	Females	Age	$\dfrac{N_x^{(12)}}{D_x}$ Males	Females
5	24.5737		52	15.0762	16.6961
6	24.4888		53	14.7419	16.3793
7	24.3998		54	14.4042	16.0587
8	24.3067		55	14.0629	15.7347
9	24.2097		56	13.7179	15.4071
10	24.1090	24.5737	57	13.3689	15.0762
11	24.0044	24.4888	58	13.0156	14.7419
12	23.8961	24.3998	59	12.6579	14.4042
13	23.7839	24.3067	60	12.2956	14.0629
14	23.6677	24.2097	61	11.9291	13.7179
15	23.5473	24.1090	62	11.5588	13.3689
16	23.4227	24.0044	63	11.1857	13.0156
17	23.2937	23.8961	64	10.8110	12.6579
18	23.1601	23.7839	65	10.4365	12.2956
19	23.0218	23.6677	66	10.0645	11.9291
20	22.8787	23.5473	67	9.6977	11.5588
21	22.7307	23.4227	68	9.3360	11.1857
22	22.5775	23.2937	69	8.9771	10.8110
23	22.4191	23.1601	70	8.6197	10.4365
24	22.2552	23.0218	71	8.2655	10.0645
25	22.0858	22.8787	72	7.9168	9.6977
26	21.9107	22.7307	73	7.5747	9.3360
27	21.7297	22.5775	74	7.2394	8.9771
28	21.5426	22.4191	75	6.9112	8.6197
29	21.3495	22.2552	76	6.5900	8.2655
30	21.1500	22.0858	77	6.2772	7.9168
31	20.9440	21.9107	78	5.9757	7.5747
32	20.7314	21.7297	79	5.6877	7.2394
33	20.5121	21.5426	80	5.4148	6.9112
34	20.2858	21.3495	81	5.1573	6.5900
35	20.0525	21.1500	82	4.9144	6.2772
36	19.8120	20.9440	83	4.6852	5.9757
37	19.5642	20.7314	84	4.4684	5.6877
38	19.3089	20.5121	85	4.2628	5.4148
39	19.0460	20.2858	86	4.0669	5.1573
40	18.7755	20.0525	87	3.8795	4.9144
41	18.4972	19.8120	88	3.6995	4.6852
42	18.2114	19.5642	89	3.5263	4.4684
43	17.9191	19.3089	90	3.3595	4.2628
44	17.6208	19.0460	91	3.1987	4.0669
45	17.3172	18.7755	92	3.0425	3.8795
46	17.0088	18.4972	93	2.8903	3.6995
47	16.6961	18.2114	94	2.7416	3.5263
48	16.3793	17.9191	95	2.5962	3.3595
49	16.0587	17.6208	96	2.4537	3.1987
50	15.7347	17.3172	97	2.3140	3.0425
51	15.4071	17.0088	98	2.1769	2.8903

PENSION RESEARCH COUNCIL STUDY—1966

DEFERRED ANNUITY RATES
(Retirement Age 65)

Age	$\dfrac{N_{65}^{(12)}}{D_x}$ Males	Females	Age	$\dfrac{N_{65}^{(12)}}{D_x}$ Males	Females
5	.8830		35	2.7211	3.5012
6	.9166		36	2.8270	3.6361
7	.9515		37	2.9373	3.7764
8	.9877		38	3.0523	3.9224
9	1.0252		39	3.1722	4.0744
10	1.0642	1.3735	40	3.2973	4.2326
11	1.1046	1.4258	41	3.4278	4.3974
12	1.1466	1.4801	42	3.5641	4.5690
13	1.1901	1.5363	43	3.7069	4.7479
14	1.2354	1.5947	44	3.8565	4.9344
15	1.2824	1.6553	45	4.0138	5.1289
16	1.3312	1.7182	46	4.1793	5.3319
17	1.3819	1.7835	47	4.3537	5.5440
18	1.4345	1.8513	48	4.5378	5.7661
19	1.4891	1.9217	49	4.7325	5.9989
20	1.5459	1.9948	50	4.9386	6.2435
21	1.6049	2.0707	51	5.1572	6.5009
22	1.6661	2.1495	52	5.3894	6.7722
23	1.7297	2.2314	53	5.6362	7.0586
24	1.7958	2.3164	54	5.8991	7.3615
25	1.8645	2.4047	55	6.1794	7.6821
26	1.9359	2.4964	56	6.4787	8.0222
27	2.0101	2.5917	57	6.7988	8.3832
28	2.0873	2.6906	58	7.1416	8.7672
29	2.1674	2.7935	59	7.5093	9.1761
30	2.2508	2.9003	60	7.9046	9.6121
31	2.3376	3.0114	61	8.3306	10.0777
32	2.4278	3.1268	62	8.7912	10.5756
33	2.5216	3.2468	63	9.2914	11.1088
34	2.6193	3.3715	64	9.8373	11.6808

PENSION RESEARCH COUNCIL STUDY—1966

Deferred Annuity Rates
(Retirement Age 62)

Age	$\dfrac{N_{62}{}^{(12)}}{D_x}$		Age	$\dfrac{N_{62}{}^{(12)}}{D_x}$	
	Males	Females		Males	Females
5	1.1610		34	3.4439	4.2620
6	1.2052		35	3.5777	4.4259
7	1.2510		36	3.7169	4.5965
8	1.2986		37	3.8620	4.7739
9	1.3479		38	4.0132	4.9585
10	1.3992	1.7363	39	4.1708	5.1506
11	1.4523	1.8024	40	4.3353	5.3506
12	1.5075	1.8710	41	4.5069	5.5589
13	1.5648	1.9421	42	4.6861	5.7758
14	1.6243	2.0159	43	4.8738	6.0019
15	1.6861	2.0925	44	5.0706	6.2377
16	1.7503	2.1720	45	5.2774	6.4836
17	1.8169	2.2546	46	5.4949	6.7402
18	1.8861	2.3403	47	5.7243	7.0083
19	1.9579	2.4292	48	5.9664	7.2890
20	2.0326	2.5217	49	6.2223	7.5833
21	2.1101	2.6176	50	6.4934	7.8926
22	2.1906	2.7172	51	6.7808	8.2179
23	2.2743	2.8207	52	7.0860	8.5609
24	2.3612	2.9282	53	7.4106	8.9230
25	2.4515	3.0398	54	7.7562	9.3058
26	2.5454	3.1557	55	8.1247	9.7112
27	2.6429	3.2762	56	8.5183	10.1410
28	2.7444	3.4013	57	8.9392	10.5974
29	2.8498	3.5313	58	9.3899	11.0828
30	2.9594	3.6664	59	9.8733	11.5997
31	3.0734	3.8067	60	10.3930	12.1509
32	3.1921	3.9526	61	10.9531	12.7395
33	3.3155	4.1043			

PENSION RESEARCH COUNCIL STUDY—1966

DEFERRED ANNUITY RATES
(Retirement Age 60)

Age	$\dfrac{N_{60}^{(12)}}{D_x}$ Males	Females	Age	$\dfrac{N_{60}^{(12)}}{D_x}$ Males	Females
5	1.3735		33	3.9224	4.7501
6	1.4258		34	4.0744	4.9326
7	1.4801		35	4.2326	5.1224
8	1.5363		36	4.3974	5.3198
9	1.5947		37	4.5690	5.5251
10	1.6553	2.0095	38	4.7479	5.7387
11	1.7182	2.0861	39	4.9344	5.9611
12	1.7835	2.1654	40	5.1289	6.1925
13	1.8513	2.2477	41	5.3319	6.4336
14	1.9217	2.3331	42	5.5440	6.6847
15	1.9948	2.4218	43	5.7661	6.9464
16	2.0707	2.5138	44	5.9989	7.2192
17	2.1495	2.6093	45	6.2435	7.5038
18	2.2314	2.7085	46	6.5009	7.8008
19	2.3164	2.8115	47	6.7722	8.1111
20	2.4047	2.9185	48	7.0586	8.4360
21	2.4964	3.0295	49	7.3615	8.7766
22	2.5917	3.1448	50	7.6821	9.1345
23	2.6906	3.2646	51	8.0222	9.5111
24	2.7935	3.3890	52	8.3832	9.9080
25	2.9003	3.5181	53	8.7672	10.3271
26	3.0114	3.6523	54	9.1761	10.7701
27	3.1268	3.7917	55	9.6121	11.2393
28	3.2468	3.9365	56	10.0777	11.7368
29	3.3715	4.0870	57	10.5756	12.2650
30	3.5012	4.2433	58	11.1088	12.8268
31	3.6361	4.4058	59	11.6808	13.4250
32	3.7764	4.5746			